Channel Islands National Park – Climate of 2011

Natural Resource Data Series NPS/MEDN/NRDS—2012/374

Michael T. Tercek, Ph.D.
Walking Shadow Ecology
PO Box 1085
Gardiner, Montana 59030

October 2012

U.S. Department of the Interior
National Park Service
Natural Resource Stewardship and Science
Fort Collins, Colorado

The National Park Service, Natural Resource Stewardship and Science office in Fort Collins, Colorado, publishes a range of reports that address natural resource topics. These reports are of interest and applicability to a broad audience in the National Park Service and others in natural resource management, including scientists, conservation and environmental constituencies, and the public.

The Natural Resource Data Series is intended for the timely release of basic data sets and data summaries. Care has been taken to assure accuracy of raw data values, but a thorough analysis and interpretation of the data has not been completed. Consequently, the initial analyses of data in this report are provisional and subject to change.

All manuscripts in the series receive the appropriate level of peer review to ensure that the information is scientifically credible, technically accurate, appropriately written for the intended audience, and designed and published in a professional manner.

This report received informal peer review by subject-matter experts who were not directly involved in the collection, analysis, or reporting of the data.

Views, statements, findings, conclusions, recommendations, and data in this report do not necessarily reflect views and policies of the National Park Service, U.S. Department of the Interior. Mention of trade names or commercial products does not constitute endorsement or recommendation for use by the U.S. Government.

This report is available from the Mediterranean Coast Network of the National Park Service (http://science.nature.nps.gov/im/units/medn/) and the Natural Resource Publications Management website (http://www.nature.nps.gov/publications/nrpm/).

Please cite this publication as:

NPS 159/117169, October 2012

Contents

	Page
Figures	v
Tables	vi
Executive Summary	vii
Acknowledgments	viii
Glossary	viii
Introduction	1
Approach and Methods	3
Selection of Datasets	3
Quality Control of Global Historical Climatology Network Data	4
Quality Control of RAWS Data	5
Analysis of Wind Data	5
Results	6
Comparison of 1971 – 2000 vs. 1981 – 2010 averages.	6
Temperature, Precipitation, and Drought Status During Calendar Year 2011	7
Broader Picture – La Nina conditions and a "late spring"	7
Annual Summary of Precipitation and Temperature	7
January – May: Highlights	8
June – August: Highlights	8
September – December: Highlights	13
Accumulated Growing Degree Days, an Index of Growing Season Length	16
Wind and Fire Risk Conditions	16
Conclusions	23
Literature Cited	24

Contents (continued)

Page

Appendix 1 25

Appendix 2 26

Appendix 3 38

Comparison of Manual vs. Automated Precipitation Measurements on Santa
Cruz, Santa Rosa and Santa Barbara Islands 38

Figures

Page

Figure 1. Map showing key climate stations in Channel Islands National Park...........................4

Figure 2. Differences between climatic "normals" (30-year averages) calculated for 1971 – 2000 vs. 1981 – 2010 on Santa Cruz Island. Monthly values are plotted on the left axis. Yearly values are on the right axis. 6

Figure 3. U.S. Drought Monitor maps for Channel Island National Park during calendar years 2010 - 2011. Drought classifications range from "abnormally dry" (D0) to "exceptional drought" (D4). White areas on the map indicate lack of drought status. 9

Figure 4. Maps showing percent of average precipitation relative to 1971–2000 for each month during 2011.. 10

Figure 5. Maps showing departures from 1971 – 2000 average daily maximum temperatures (Tmax) in degrees Fahrenheit. Estimates are from the Parameter-elevation Regressions on Independent Slopes Model (PRISM). Gray areas = Pacific Ocean. 11

Figure 6. Maps showing departures from 1971 – 2000 average daily minimum temperatures (Tmin) in degrees Fahrenheit. Estimates are from the Parameter-elevation Regressions on Independent Slopes Model (PRISM). Gray areas = Pacific Ocean.. 12

Figure 7. Departure of 2011 precipitation from 30-year averages on Santa Cruz Island in Channel Islands National Park.. 18

Figure 8. Total monthly precipitation, average daily maximum temperature (Tmax), and average daily minimum temperature (Tmin) for the period of record at automated (RAWS) stations in Channel Islands National Park. 19

Figure 9. Wind roses for RAWS stations in Channel Islands National Park, contrasting calendar year 2011 to the averages for 2005 – 2010.. 20

Figure 10. The Keetch-Byram Drought Index (KBDI) calculated for every day during the period of record for the Santa Cruz Island weather station.................................... 22

Appendix 3, Figure 1. Comparison of precipitation measurements from manual vs. automated weather stations in Channel Islands National Park. 39

Tables

Page

Table 1. Monthly precipitation in inches during 2011 in Channel Islands National Park. For Santa Cruz Island Main Ranch, departures from 1971 – 2000 and 1981 - 2010 averages (%) are shown in parenthesis. 14

Table 2. Average daily maximum temperatures (Tmax) and average daily minimum temperatures (Tmin) during 2011. 15

Table 3. Accumulated Growing Degree Days (AGDD) and days above or below critical temperature thresholds during 2011. (-) = insufficient data for an accurate calculation. 17

Executive Summary

This report details the climate (temperature, precipitation, drought, and wind conditions) of Channel Island National Park (NP) during 2011. Gridded maps are used to present broad-brush conditions across the region for each month. This regional presentation is compared to detailed data from Remote Automated Weather Stations (RAWS), and weather stations in the Global Historical Climatology Network. Prior to analysis, a set of data quality control checks were performed by the author in accordance with established an National Park Service protocol (Rocky Mountain Climate Working Group 2010). Key points summarizing calendar year 2011 are presented as bullets in the Conclusion section at the end of the report. There was significant spatial and month to month variability in the data that provided exceptions to these generalizations, so an examination of the regional maps (Figs. 4-6) are key to understanding the climatic patterns for 2011. The Results section contains a narratives that provides details for each season of the year. Readers can download the data used in this report and make custom climate graphs and tables of their own by visiting www.ClimateAnalyzer.org

Acknowledgments

Funding for this report was provided by National Park Service Mediterranean Coast Network Inventory and Monitoring Program.

Glossary

GHCN – Global Historical Climatology Network.

RAWS – Remote Automated Weather Station

PRISM - Parameter-elevation Regression on Independent Slopes Model. See
http://www.prism.oregonstate.edu/

US Drought Monitor - A broad brush assessment of drought conditions. See
http://drought.unl.edu/dm/monitor.html

B-91 Forms – Paper data sheets that are used to record climate data at weather stations

Tmax / Tmin – mean daily Maximum / Minimum Temperatures

NOAA - National Oceanic and Atmospheric Administration

30-year average or "normal" – Official 30-year averages for each weather station are issued every 10 years by NOAA. Prior to 2011, the official reference period was 1971 – 2000. Because 2011 was the first year in which 1981 – 2010 averages were in widespread use, both reference periods were used in this report.

Introduction

This report details the climate (temperature, precipitation, drought, and wind conditions) of Channel Islands National Park (NP) during 2011. Climatic events are presented both from a local perspective, with data from individual weather stations, and from a regional perspective, with maps that depict broad-scale conditions across southern California during each month of the year. The climatic conditions of 2011 are also compared to a historical context, based primarily on a 30-year average or "normal" period.

Typically, when a weather report states that a particular month was "warmer than average" or "cooler than normal," the comparison is to a set of averages calculated over an agreed upon time period. These averages, which are known as "climatological normals," are updated every 10 years by the National Oceanic and Atmospheric Administration (NOAA). From 1991 – 2000, meteorological measurements were compared to 1961 – 1990 averages; from 2001 – 2010 the reference period was 1971 – 2000; and starting in calendar year 2011, most weather data will be compared to 1981 – 2010 averages. NOAA further defines climatological normals as follows:

"In the strictest sense, a "normal" of a particular variable (e.g., temperature) is defined as the 30-year average. For example, the minimum temperature normal in January for a station in Chicago, Illinois, would be computed by taking the average of the 30 January values of monthly-averaged minimum temperatures from 1981 to 2010. Each of the 30 monthly values was in turn derived from averaging the daily observations of minimum temperature for the station. In practice, however, much more goes into NCDC's Normals product than simple 30-year averages. Procedures are put in place to deal with missing and suspect data values. In addition, Normals include quantities other than averages such as degree days, probabilities, standard deviations, etc. Normals are a large suite of data products that provide users with many tools to understand typical climate conditions for thousands of locations across the United States." (Source: http://www.ncdc.noaa.gov/oa/climate/normals/usnormals.html#WHATARENORMALS)

Since 2011 was the first year in which 1981 – 2010 averages were commonly used, most of the climate parameters in this report are compared to both 1971 – 2000 and 1981 – 2010 averages. If this approach had not been taken, it would have been difficult to compare this report to its predecessor (Tercek 2011), which summarized the climate of Channel Islands NP during 2010. This is because a precipitation measurement that would have been considered below average (for example, during March) when compared to the 1971 – 2000 averages, might instead be near normal when compared to the 1981 – 2010 averages. The differences between these two time periods are described in more detail in the results section.

The content in this report is divided into two sections that discuss: (1) precipitation, temperature and drought, and (2) wind and fire risk conditions. The section on temperature, precipitation and drought is further sub-divided into seasonal narratives that highlight key data and events. Those interested in additional climate-related information for Channel Island NP and the surrounding areas should seek:

Western Regional Climate Center (http://www.wrcc.dri.edu/)

Drought Monitor (http://drought.unl.edu/dm/monitor.html)

NOAA (National Oceanic Atmospheric Administration) National Weather Service
(http://www.cpc.ncep.noaa.gov/)

USGS (U.S. Geological Survey) Water National Information System
(http://waterdata.usgs.gov/nwis)

Approach and Methods

Selection of Datasets
In order to place Channel Islands NP within a regional context, grid-based estimates of precipitation and temperature were used to provide a broad overview of climatic conditions in the area. These estimates were generated with a statistical modeling technique that interpolates precipitation and temperature values between actual climate stations while also accounting for the effects of aspect and elevation. Known as the Parameter-elevation Regression on Independent Slopes Model (PRISM; http://www.prism.oregonstate.edu/), this approach has a long history of use in the western United States, and it has been shown to provide robust products in a wide variety of studies (Daly et al. 2008). At the time of writing, 1981 – 2010 averages (normals) were not available for PRISM data, so 1971 – 2000 PRISM normals were used.

Records from individual precipitation and temperature observing stations were included as a way to highlight intra-regional variability. The process of selecting specific stations included in this report is described in the Rocky Mountain Climate Protocol (Rocky Mountain Climate Working Group 2010). Generally, the selection criteria were:

1. Stations provide good spatial coverage within and near the parks of interest. In the case of Channel Islands NP, RAWS stations were chosen because they are located within the administrative boundaries of the park (Fig. 1) and are routinely consulted by NPS staff. In addition, National Weather Service (NWS, "Ranger") stations were chosen because they have long, established records that can be meaningfully compared to the RAWS stations. Data from the NWS stations are available through the Global Historical Climatology Network (GHCN). NWS/GHCN stations have several advantages, including their relatively long period of record (Appendix 1), and the availability of established 30-year averages that can be used to quantify the difference between the current year and "normal" conditions.

2. Stations provide a sufficient length of record to provide historical context for current observations.

3. Instrumentation at individual stations is relatively consistent over the life of the record.

4. Instrumentation and siting standards used in selected networks are suitable for providing consistent, continuous, and long-duration records of climate.

As a way of presenting the integrated effects of temperature and precipitation, maps from the US Drought Monitor (http://drought.unl.edu/dm/monitor.html) were used to depict broad-brush conditions across the region. To present more fine-scale drought conditions, the Keetch-Byram Drought Index (KBDI) was calculated for every day during the period of record at select weather stations in the region. Methods for these calculations were based on Alexander (1990), who identified typographical errors in the original Keetch-Byram (1968) description of the index. The KBDI can be interpreted as the amount of precipitation (expressed in hundredths of inches) that would be needed to restore the soil to full capacity. A KBDI index of zero indicates soil saturation, and a KBDI of 800 indicates maximum possible drought, in which, theoretically, 8 or more inches of rain would be needed to replenish the soil (Keetch and Byram 1968). The KBDI is used in fire modeling and has been shown to be a good predictor of conditions that favor fires that burn deeply into the organic soil layers, thus making them more resistant to control efforts (Dolling et al. 2005).

The locations of weather stations cited in this report are shown in Figure 1. Metadata for these stations can be accessed from the internet links provided in Appendix 1.

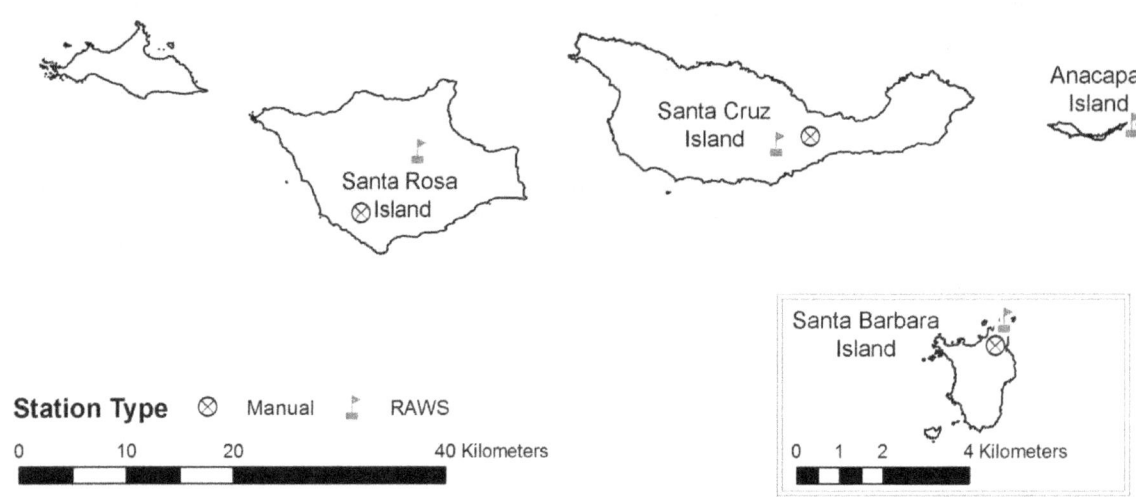

Figure 1. Map showing key climate stations in Channel Islands National Park.

Quality Control of Global Historical Climatology Network Data

As of January 2012, weather station data are no longer available from the internet in the Cooperative Observer Program (COOP) format, and this format is not expected to return "any time soon" (National Climatic Data Center, personal communication to author). All of the weather stations that were served by this data portal have been transferred to the Global Historical Climatology Network (GHCN), which is available online at this address: http://www.ncdc.noaa.gov/cdo-web/search.

In addition to using metric units, different methods of expressing missing values, and a different row / column arrangement of values, this format also employs a new set of data quality flags that indicate the level of confidence in each measurement and any modifications that were made to each data point during routine Qa/Qc by the National Weather Service. In response to these changes, the author of this report has created software tools that assist in the interpretation of the data flags and diagnostic plotting of the data. Following guidelines from Kittel (2008), Kittel et al. (2009), and Rocky Mountain Climate Working Group (2010), the Qa/Qc employed by these software tools involved graphing and visual inspection of each time series, evaluation of the data quality flags that accompany each observation, comparison with historical observations and observations from surrounding sites, and logical consistency tests (e.g., confirming that minimum daily temperatures were lower than the daily maximum temperatures). Point

4

observations provided by the GHCN stations were also compared to corresponding estimates from the PRISM datasets and to the original datasheets (B-91 forms) used by weather station staff. When possible, data missing in the electronic records were recovered from the original datasheets and hand entered by the author of this report. If more than 3 days of precipitation data were missing for a particular month, a monthly total was not calculated, and the entire month was instead considered missing. Similarly, if more than 5 days of mean daily maximum temperature (Tmax) or mean daily minimum temperature (Tmin) were missing, monthly average temperatures were not calculated. The data handling was conservative, i.e., no data points were changed unless it was very clear that an erroneous value, for example a precipitation measurement with a missing decimal point that could be verified on the original station records, was found. To download the software used for data screening and to learn more about the methods, visit www.YellowstoneEcology.com. Readers can download the data used in this report and make custom climate graphs and tables of their own by visiting www.ClimateAnalyzer.org

Quality Control of RAWS Data

Because RAWS data are collected hourly, daily Tmax, Tmin, and precipitation values must be derived from the automated data stream. Furthermore, precipitation is recorded as a running total that must be translated into daily measurements. If any particular day in a record was missing more than two hours of measurements, the entire day was considered missing. In addition, if the temperature during any day varied by less than 2 degrees Fahrenheit, data for the entire day was considered invalid due to instrumental error and replaced with missing values. Once daily statistics had been calculated, diagnostic plots were used to screen for physically impossible measurements, which were ascribed to instrumental error and considered missing; and the missing data criteria just described for GHCN stations were used to calculate monthly statistics.

All the data used in the preparation of this report (including original and quality checked files) are available electronically from the Mediterranean Coast Network I&M program. These data files may be read and re-analyzed by the same software that was used to produce this report, available for download at www.YellowstoneEcology.com.

Analysis of Wind Data

Wind roses were used to present average conditions during 2011 and to contrast them with the period 2005 – 2010. This period was chosen because it was common to all the RAWS stations in the study area. More details for each month of 2011 are presented in Appendix 2.

Results

Comparison of 1971 – 2000 vs. 1981 – 2010 averages.

Since much of this report is based on a comparison between the current year and official monthly averages based on a 30-year period (see the Introduction), it is useful to be aware of the changes in these averages when the reference period is updated. Since 2011 was the first year in which 1981 – 2010 was the standard 30 –year reference period, Figure 2 shows the differences between the current period and 1971 – 2000 (the previous reference period). This station does not record temperature. Precipitation averages for February, April, October, and December were greater during 1981 – 2010. March average precipitation was lower during 1981 – 2010, and other months had smaller changes in precipitation. The same differences in monthly values were observed on the mainland, at the UCLA and Santa Monica Pier weather stations (see the companion report "Climate of 2011 – Santa Monica Mountains National Recreation Area). Overall, these changes are slight and it is not possible at this time to determine whether they are the result of natural variability or climate change. Throughout the text of this report, all departures from the 30-year average are referenced to 1981 – 2010, but the tables and graphs provide comparisons to both periods.

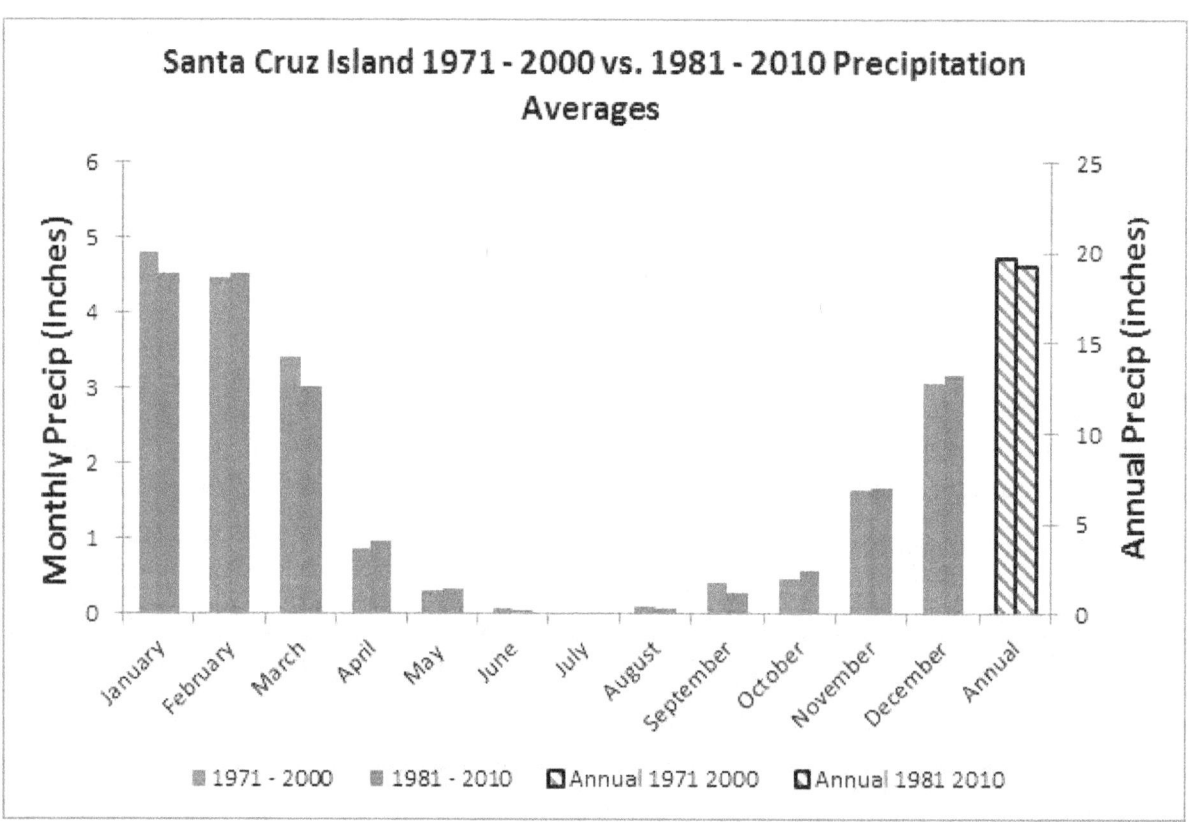

Figure 2. Differences between climatic "normals" (30-year averages) calculated for 1971 – 2000 vs. 1981 – 2010 on Santa Cruz Island. Monthly values are plotted on the left axis. Yearly values are on the right axis.

Temperature, Precipitation, and Drought Status During Calendar Year 2011

The patterns described in this section are often stated as broad generalizations. In most cases there was significant variability across the region and exceptions to the patterns described here were common. In order to appreciate this variability, it is important to examine the PRISM maps (Figures 4 – 6) and compare them to the weather station data presented in the Figures 7 – 9 and Tables 1 – 2.

Broader Picture – La Nina conditions and a "late spring"

The El Nino – Southern Oscillation (ENSO) is an oscillation of the ocean – atmosphere climate system centered over the tropical Pacific Ocean that follows a rough cycle of approximately 2 – 7 years. When ENSO is in its "El Nino phase," sea surface temperatures in the central and eastern tropical Pacific are warmer than average, and this generally produces warmer, drier conditions in the northern continental United States and cooler, wetter conditions in the southern United States, particularly the southwest. In contrast, the opposite conditions prevail when ENSO is in its "La Nina phase." More information on ENSO can be found on the NOAA web site located here: http://www.pmel.noaa.gov/tao/elnino/el-nino-story.html ENSO interacts with another climatological cycle known as the Pacific Decadal Oscillation (PDO), which has similar effects on weather in the United States but cycles over roughly 10 – 30 years. More information on the PDO can be obtained from NOAA here: http://www.ncdc.noaa.gov/teleconnections/pdo/

During 2011, ENSO was in a strong La Nina phase and the PDO was in a cool phase that should have reinforced the La Nina effects on climate. For long-term El Nino patterns, consult NOAA here: http://www.cpc.ncep.noaa.gov/products/analysis_monitoring/ensostuff/ensoyears.shtml

Normally, La Nina conditions would produce drier conditions in southern California. However, in the case of the 2010 - 2011 winter, the expected La Nina effects were not clearly seen. Rather than being dry, December 2010 had roughly 350% normal precipitation on Santa Cruz Island (see Tercek 2011 for more details), and the Channel Islands had a very wet spring. Traditionally, a rough dividing line between "northern" and "southern" California, in this context, might be drawn near Point Conception, which is not very far north of Channel Islands National Park. Perhaps because it is near the "north," or perhaps because of other factors, Channel Islands National Park had some of the highest May and June precipitation on record, in contrast to inland locations and locations further south. June 2011 was the third wettest recorded on Santa Cruz Island since 1904, with roughly 3100% the 1981 – 2010 average, and May 2011 was about 700% average. In contrast, the UCLA weather station on the mainland had only 36% average precipitation during June and the San Diego airport had 35% of the 1981 – 2010 average precipitation for June. The difference between the islands and more inland locations can also be seen in the PRISM maps that are presented in the next section of this report (see the June panel of Figure 4). The late, wet spring seen in the Channel Islands during 2011 resembled the pattern seen throughout the Pacific Northwest and the northern continental US. Compare to the national summary of 2011 provided by NOAA here: http://www.ncdc.noaa.gov/sotc/national/2011/13

Annual Summary of Precipitation and Temperature

After recovering from drought during 2010, the region remained drought free for the entirety of calendar year 2011 (Figure 3). This was true despite below average precipitation during January, April, September, and December (Figure 4). Total precipitation for the year at Santa Cruz Island Main Ranch was 19.59 inches, which was 99.8% average. Temperatures were generally near to below the 30-year averages throughout much of the region, with the exception of January and April, which were in some places 2 or more degrees (F) above average. Remote Automated Weather Stations (RAWS) on the Channel Islands recorded generally above average precipitation and average to below average temperatures (Figure 8). Highlights of interest for each season are described below. See Figures 4 – 8 and Tables 1 – 2 for more details.

January – May: Highlights.
Quick Summary: The region remained drought free because dry and warm conditions during January and February were compensated by wetter than average conditions in March and May. April was drier than average but had near normal temperatures.

More Detail: Temperatures were generally above average during January, and precipitation was well below average during both January and February (Figures 4 -6). Santa Cruz Island precipitation was 27% the 1981 – 2010 averages during January and 61% average during February (Table 1). The automated stations on Santa Rosa and Anacapa Islands recorded some of the highest temperatures in their record during January (Figure 8) but most of the region was only 1 – 2 degrees above average during January (Figures 4, 5). March had generally above average precipitation, with temperatures that were generally near average. April precipitation was generally less than 25% the 30-year averages throughout the region (Figure 4) and only 4% average on Santa Cruz Island (Table 1). May had generally above average precipitation throughout the region (Figure 4), and on Santa Cruz Island May precipitation was remarkably high –700% the 1981 – 2010 average. See Figures 4 – 8 and Tables 1 – 2 for more details.

June – August: Highlights
Quick Summary: The region typically has low precipitation during the summer, but June was unusual because of its very great rainfall. Temperatures ranged from near average to below average.

More Detail: Weather stations in the region typically record very little precipitation during June – August. For example, June average precipitation during 1981 – 2010 on Santa Cruz Island was only 0.07 inches, while July and August averages were 0.02 and 0.1 inches, respectively. In contrast, June 2011 precipitation on Santa Cruz Island was 1.88 inches, or 3100% the 1981 – 2010 averages. It was the third wettest June on Santa Cruz Island since records began in 1904.

Because average ("normal") precipitation is low during these months, care should be taken when interpreting statistics that quantify the amount (%) of normal precipitation that fell during the summer months. For example, during 2011 PRISM precipitation maps (Fig. 4) show very complex patterns during July and August, with some parts of the region experiencing very dry (0-25% average) and others very wet (>200% average). It is important to keep in mind that the absolute difference in precipitation (expressed as inches of rain rather than percent average) was very small. An example from the mainland illustrates this. At the UCLA weather station 0.04 inches of rain during June was only 36% of the 1971 – 2000 average, but if only an additional 0.07 inches of rain had fallen, the measurements would have been approximately 100% normal.

8

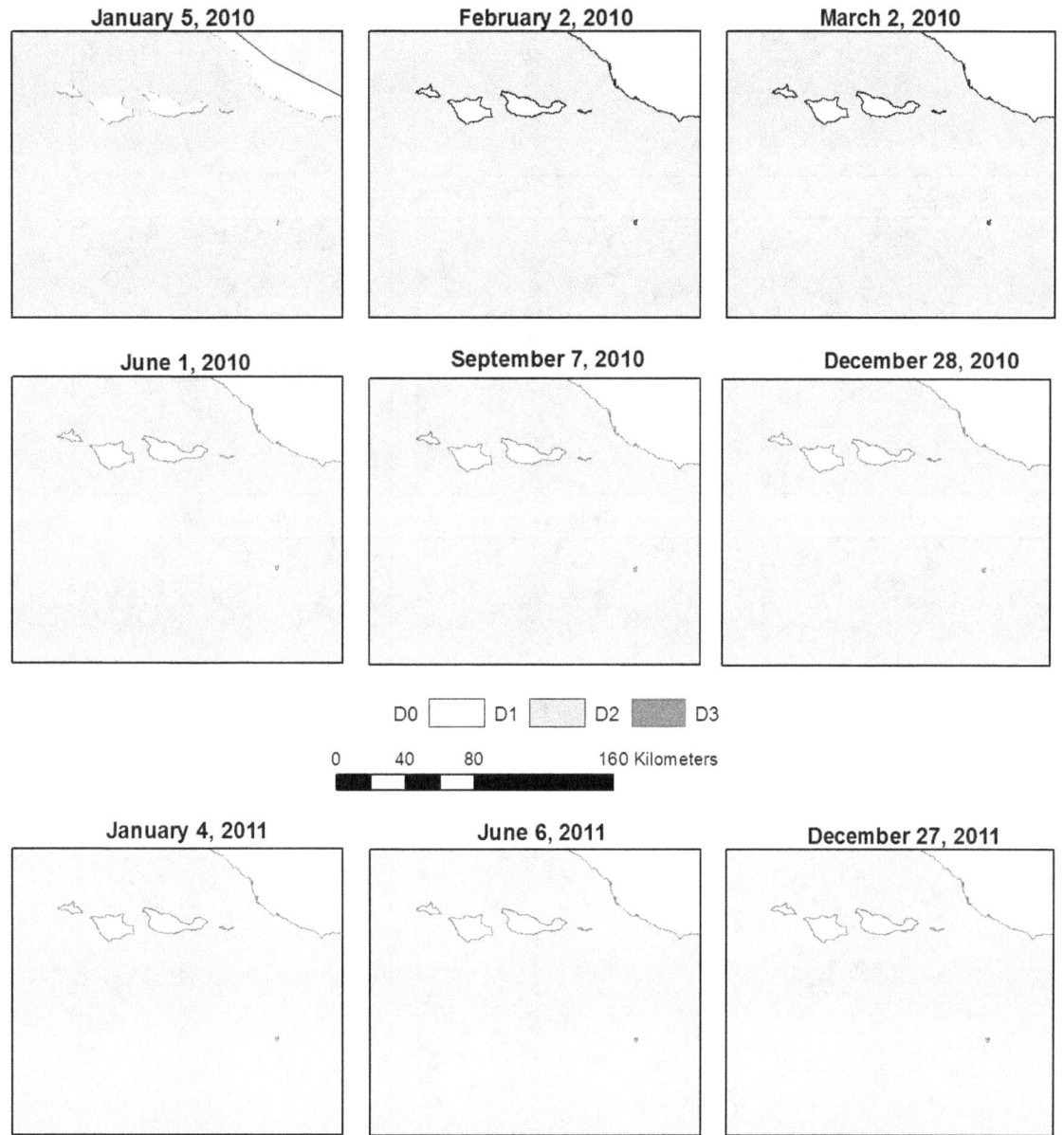

Figure 3. U.S. Drought Monitor maps for Channel Island National Park during calendar years 2010 - 2011. Drought classifications range from "abnormally dry" (D0) to "exceptional drought" (D4). White areas on the map indicate lack of drought status. For more information visit: www.drought.unl.edu/dm/monitor.html

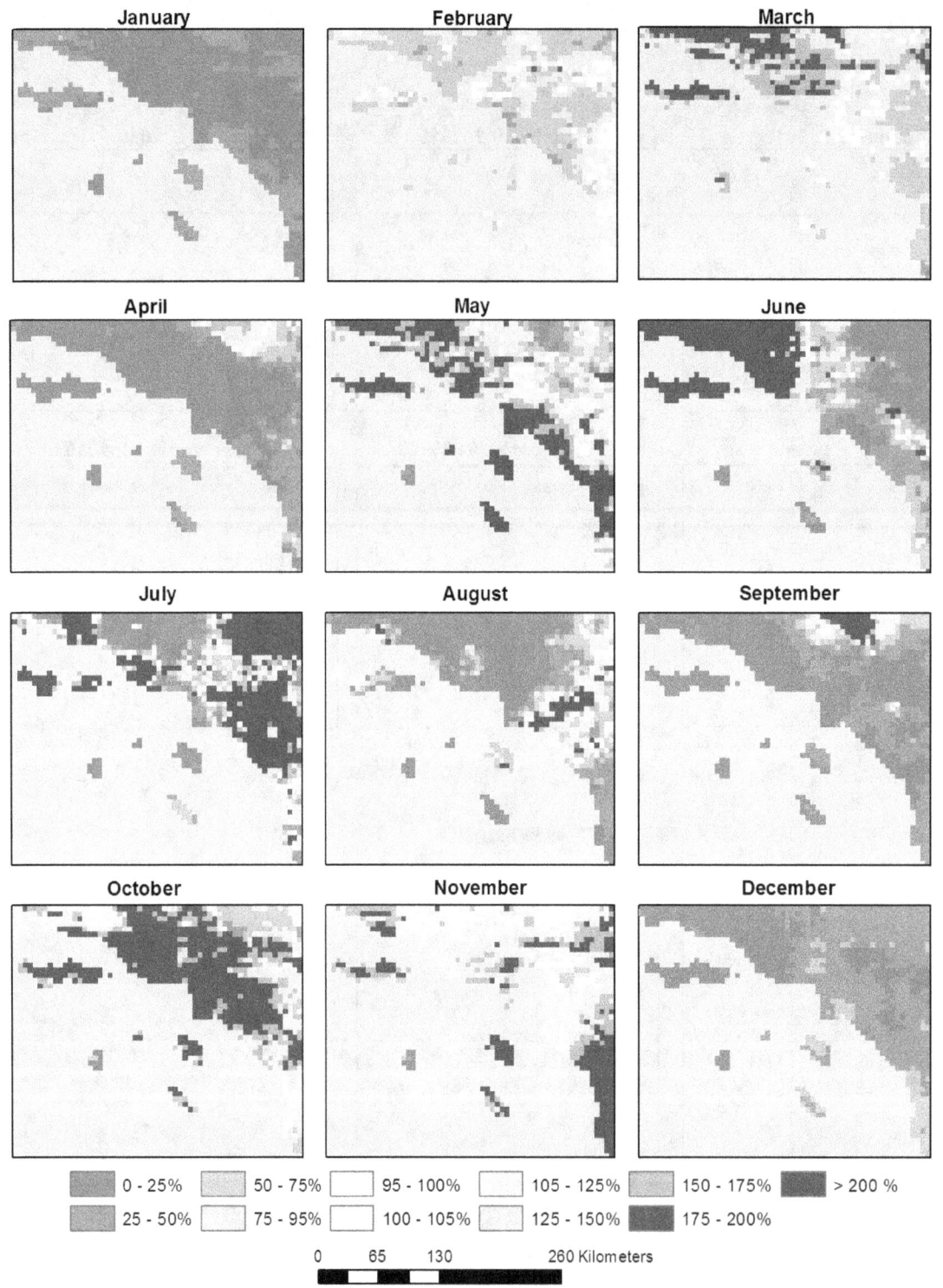

Figure 4. Maps showing percent of average precipitation relative to 1971–2000 for each month during 2011. Estimates are from the Parameter-elevation Regressions on Independent Slopes Model (PRISM). Gray areas = Pacific Ocean. For more information, see http://www.prism.oregonstate.edu/. Asterisks indicate months that had very low average precipitation during 1971 – 2000. For example, key weather stations in this region have monthly average precipitation during summer months ranging 0.01 – 0.2 inches (see Fig. 5). For this reason, map colors indicating 0 – 25% average precipitation may represent very small absolute departure from average (0.01 – 0.2 inches less than normal).

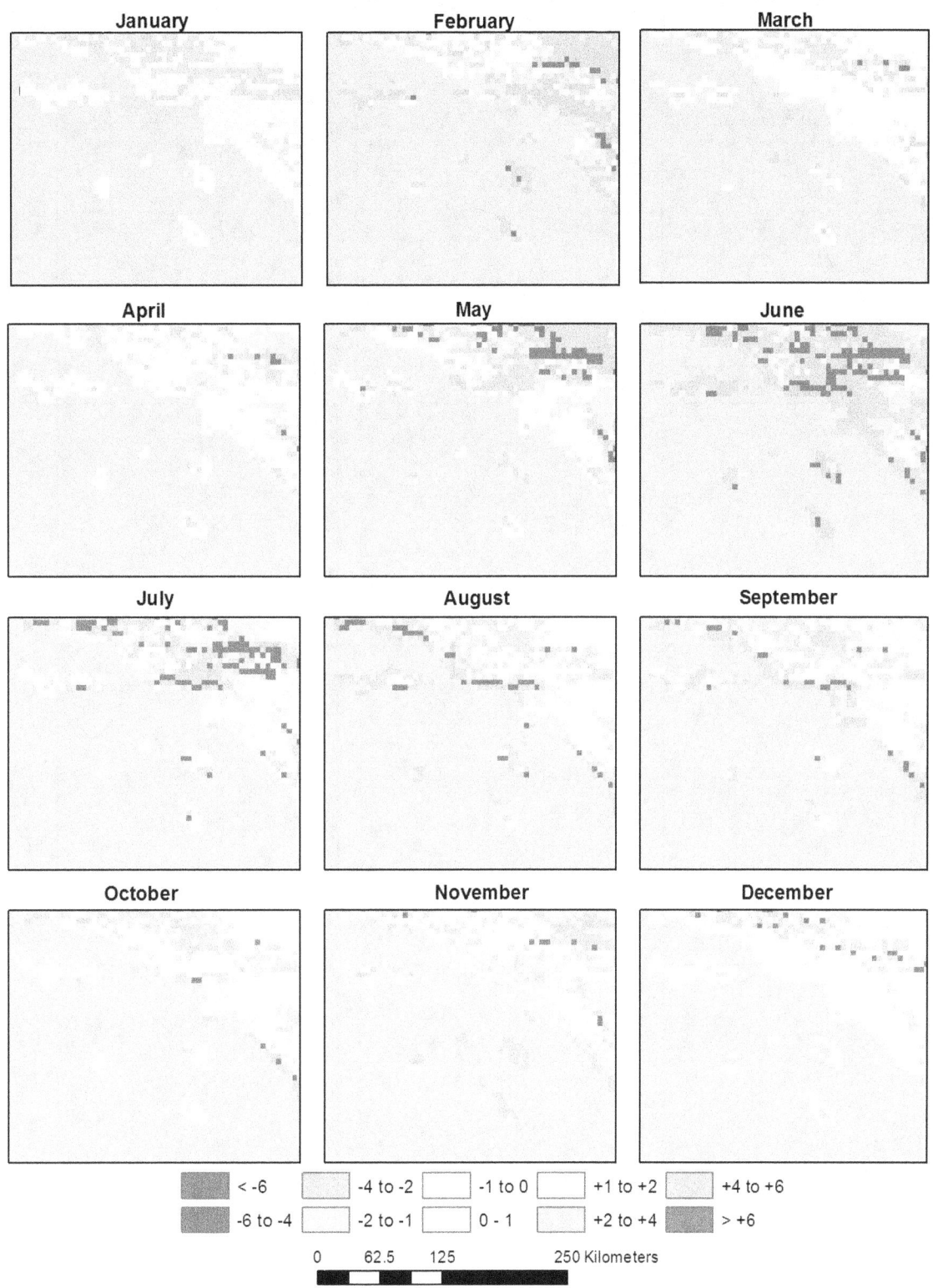

Figure 5. Maps showing departures from 1971 – 2000 average daily maximum temperatures (Tmax) in degrees Fahrenheit. Estimates are from the Parameter-elevation Regressions on Independent Slopes Model (PRISM). Gray areas = Pacific Ocean. For more information, see http://www.prism.oregonstate.edu/.

11

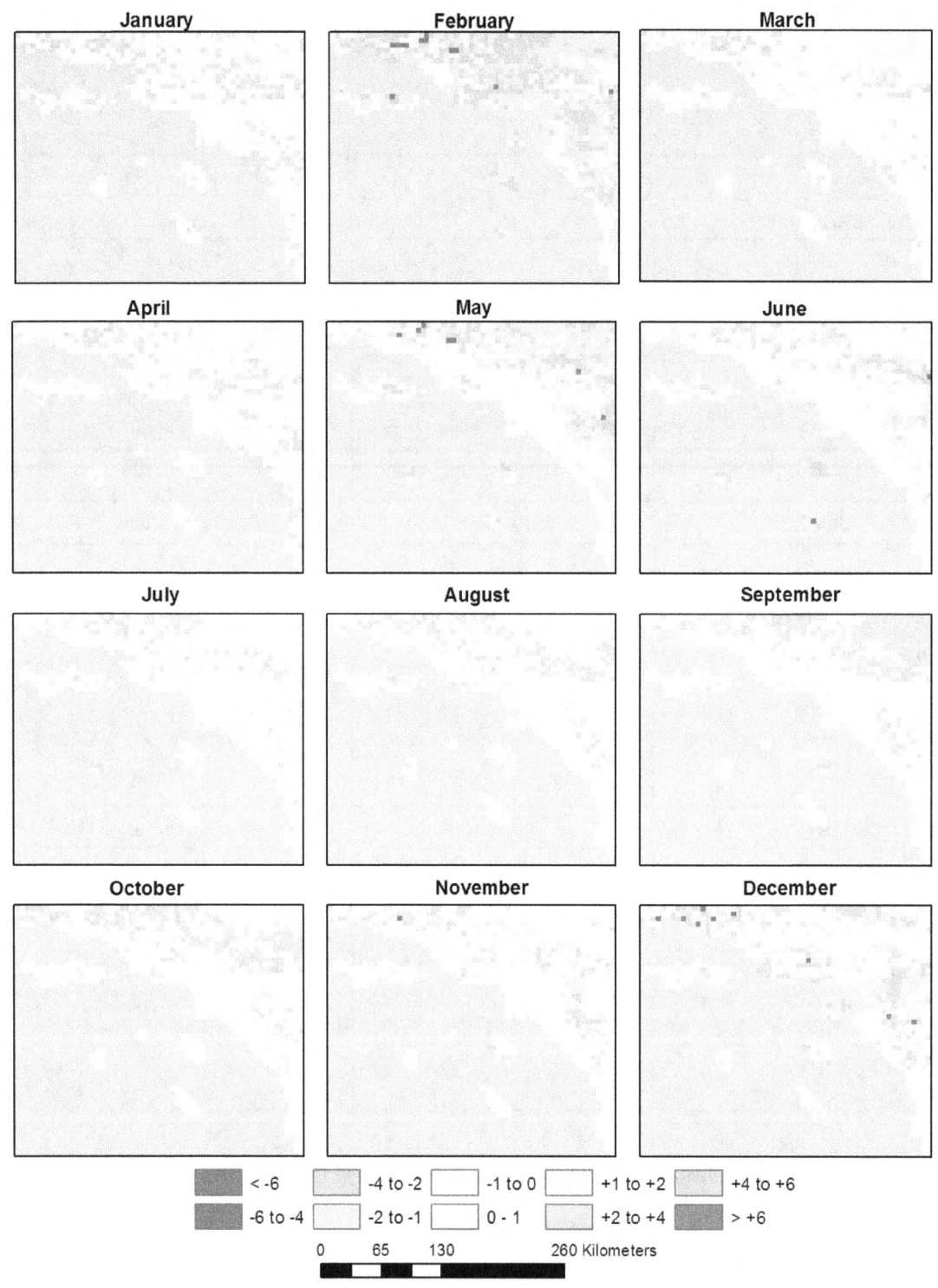

Figure 6. Maps showing departures from 1971 – 2000 average daily minimum temperatures (Tmin) in degrees Fahrenheit. Estimates are from the Parameter-elevation Regressions on Independent Slopes Model (PRISM). Gray areas = Pacific Ocean. For more information, see http://www.prism.oregonstate.edu/.

For the reasons just described, most of the "patchiness" in the PRISM precipitation maps (Figure 4) during July – August (particularly July) can be explained by the region's characteristically low summer rainfall. Temperatures during June – August were generally below average (Figures 5 – 6), with automated stations (Figure 8) recording traces in the mid-low range of their record. See Figures 4 – 8 and Tables 1 – 2 for more details.

September – December: Highlights

Quick Summary: September and December precipitation was generally less than 50% the 30 – year averages (Figure 4). October and November precipitation was generally 150% or more the 30-year averages (Figure 4, Table 1). Temperatures were generally near to below the 30-year averages.

More Detail: Santa Cruz Island reported 2% the 1981 – 2010 average during September and roughly 50% average during December (Table 1, Figure 7). In contrast, Santa Cruz Island precipitation was more than 200% the 30-year averages during both October and November (Table 1). Unlike weather stations on the mainland (e.g. UCLA), average or "normal" precipitation during October did not change greatly on Santa Cruz Island from 1971 – 2000 vs. 1981 – 2010. During October – December, the automated weather station on Santa Barbara Island recorded temperatures that were low relative to the rest of the record but the other islands had temperatures in the mid-range of their records (Figure 8).

Table 1. Monthly precipitation in inches during 2011 in Channel Islands National Park. For Santa Cruz Island Main Ranch, departures from 1971 – 2000 and 1981 - 2010 averages (%) are shown in parenthesis.

Station Name	Station Type	JAN	FEB	MAR	APR	MAY	JUN	JUL	AUG	SEP	OCT	NOV	DEC	TOT.
Santa Cruz Island	RAWS	1.23	2.27	3.99	0.02	2.55	1.59	0	0	0	1.2	3.35	1.18	17.38
Santa Cruz Island Central Valley (Main Ranch)	Manual	1.23	2.75	4.93	0.04	2.5	1.88	0 (*)	0 (*)	0.01	1.02	3.58	1.65	19.59
	% of 1971 - 2000, 1981 - 2010 averages**	25.6, 27.2	61.7, 60.8	145, 164	4.6, 4.2	806, 714	2685, 3133	(-)		2.4, 3.5	217, 214	218, 214	54, 52	100, 102
Santa Rosa Island	Manual	2.96	2.74	5.34	0.06	0	0.09	0	0	0	0.34	3.99	0.46	15.98
Santa Barbara Island	Manual	(-)	(-)	(-)	(-)	(-)	(-)	(-)	(-)	(-)	(-)	(-)	(-)	(-)
Anacapa Island	RAWS	0.86	1.51	2.61	0	0.51	0.15	0	0 0.0	0.07	0.53	2.06	0.52	8.82
Santa Rosa Island	RAWS	1.78	1.6	3.36	0.17	0.26	0.66	0.02	3	0.01	0.2	3.32	0.37	11.78
Santa Barbara Island	RAWS	0.32	0.59	1.58	0.01	0.36	0	0	0	0	0.25	2.38	0.29	5.78

Notes: For RAWS stations, daily values are not calculated if more than two hours of measurement are missing. Subsequently, monthly statistics are not reported if more than 3 days of data are missing. (-) = insufficient data.* 1971 – 2000 average precipitation at the Santa Cruz Island Main Ranch was 0.02 and 0.1 inches during July and August, respectively. ** The first % in entry parenthesis is % of 1971 - 2000 average. The second is % of 1981 - 2010 averages. If departure from 30-year averages for a particular station is not reported, there is insufficient record to calculate the average.

14

Table 2. Average daily maximum temperatures (Tmax) and average daily minimum temperatures (Tmin) during 2011.

Station Name	Station Type	Parameter	JAN	FEB	MAR	APR	MAY	JUN	JUL	AUG	SEP	OCT	NOV	DEC	YR
Santa Cruz Island	RAWS	Tmax	66.52	60.50	67.94	72.40	71.87	72.27	80.32	81.58	79.50	79.61	69.27	68.03	72.48
		Tmin	44.23	40.82	44.84	46.90	46.97	48.97	53.61	53.19	53.10	50.61	44.27	38.26	47.15
Anacapa Island	RAWS	Tmax	64.35	63.04	64.48	67.23	81.61	75.00	67.23	66.19	70.87	72.23	67.50	62.00	68.48
		Tmin	53.06	52.39	56.06	58.13	70.29	66.40	59.13	58.42	61.07	61.84	58.17	52.84	58.98
Santa Rosa Island	RAWS	Tmax	64.58	58.18	57.48	57.07	58.94	60.20	65.52	63.65	69.97	70.52	62.23	61.81	62.51
		Tmin	49.74	44.54	45.74	45.00	46.48	48.30	52.68	50.81	53.47	54.23	49.67	46.61	48.94
Santa Barbara Island	RAWS	Tmax	61.94	59.32	58.13	59.03	61.00	63.00	66.19	66.13	66.20	64.32	61.87	59.77	62.24
		Tmin	51.39	49.46	50.68	52.73	52.97	55.03	58.90	58.77	58.97	57.52	53.73	51.52	54.31

Note: For RAWS stations, daily values are not calculated if more than two hours of measurement are missing. Subsequently, monthly statistics are not reported if more than 5 days of data are missing.

Accumulated Growing Degree Days, an Index of Growing Season Length

Accumulated Growing Degree Days (AGDD) are often used as an index of growing season length. They are calculated as the sum of the differences between the average temperature for each day of the year and a base temperature. This base temperature is often chosen as the threshold below which plants are thought to be metabolically inactive. In the case of AGDD 40, the base temperature is 40 degrees Fahrenheit. Consequently, 40 is subtracted from the mean temperature for each day, and these differences are added up for the entire year, giving a single number. Similarly, AGDD 50 is calculated with a base temperature of 50 (F).

When viewed from the perspective of growing season length, calendar-year 2011 was near average to below average. AGDD 40 and AGDD 50 were 94 – 107% the averages calculated for the RAWS stations on the Island (Table 3).

Wind and Fire Risk Conditions

Summary wind data suggest that calendar-year 2011 was similar to 2005 – 2010 (Figure 9). Recorded winds were slowest on Santa Cruz Island. More details for each month of the year are presented in Appendix 2.

The Keetch – Byram Drought Index (KBDI; see Methods above), calculated for every day during the period of record at the Santa Cruz Island weather station, indicated that 2011 had low fire risk (Figure 10). The maximum value possible for KBDI is 800, which would indicate that 8 hundredths of an inch (8 inches) of water would be required to replenish the soil to field capacity. The index is commonly used to measure the probability that a fire already started would continue to burn, particularly into the deep soil layers (Keetch and Byram 1968, Alexander 1990). Seasonal patterns in KBDI at this station were similar to patterns at other weather stations in the park (not shown). Drought/fire risk was highest during the summer, when regional precipitation was at a minimum. This index can be calculated automatically on a near-real-time basis as a prediction tool. Contact the Mediterranean Coast Network Inventory and Monitoring Program to obtain the computer code that was used for these calculations.

Table 3. Accumulated Growing Degree Days (AGDD) and days above or below critical temperature thresholds during 2011. (-) = insufficient data for an accurate calculation.

Station Name	Station Type	AGDD40	AGDD50	# days >= 80 F	# days >= 90 F	# days <= 32F
Santa Cruz Island	RAWS	7256	3710	76	11	2
	Average 1990 - 2010	7008	3471	73	12	4
Anacapa Island	RAWS	8672	5022	28	3	0
	Average	(-)	(-)	(-)	(-)	(-)
Santa Rosa Island	RAWS	5752	2288	19	3	0
	Average 1990 - 2010	5779	2377	(-)	(-)	(-)
Santa Barbara Island	RAWS	6679	3039	1	0	0
	Average 1999 - 2010	6891	3244	2	0	0

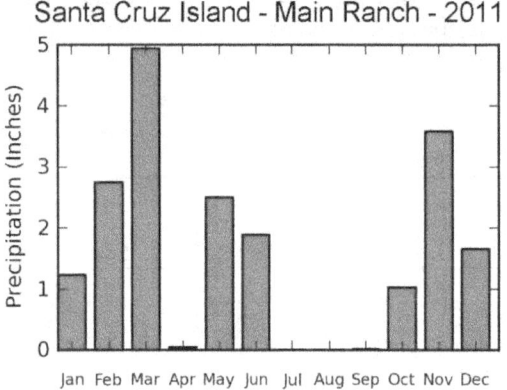

Santa Cruz Island - Main Ranch - 2011

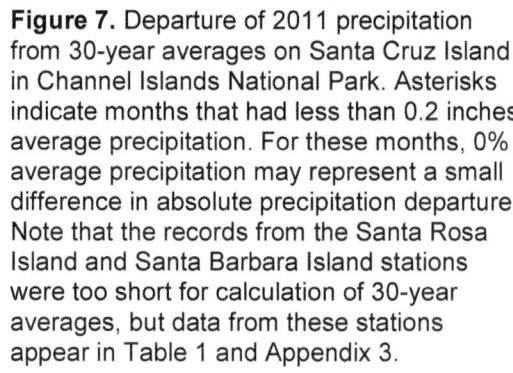

Figure 7. Departure of 2011 precipitation from 30-year averages on Santa Cruz Island in Channel Islands National Park. Asterisks indicate months that had less than 0.2 inches average precipitation. For these months, 0% average precipitation may represent a small difference in absolute precipitation departure. Note that the records from the Santa Rosa Island and Santa Barbara Island stations were too short for calculation of 30-year averages, but data from these stations appear in Table 1 and Appendix 3.

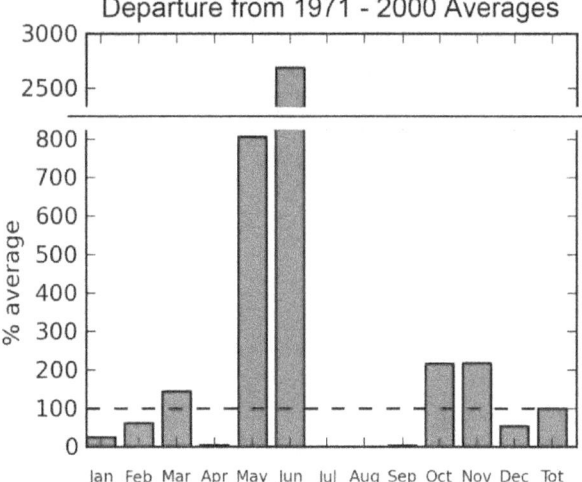

Departure from 1971 - 2000 Averages

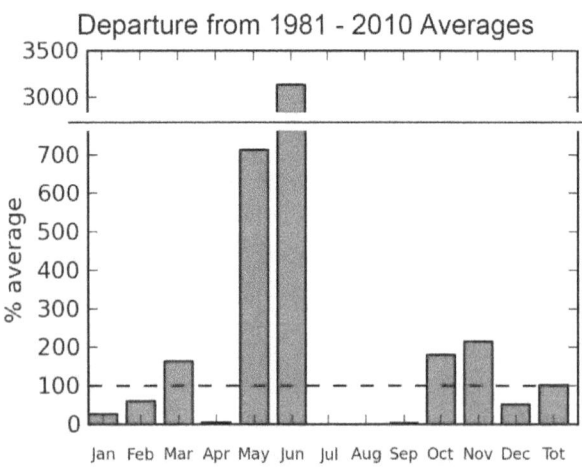

Departure from 1981 - 2010 Averages

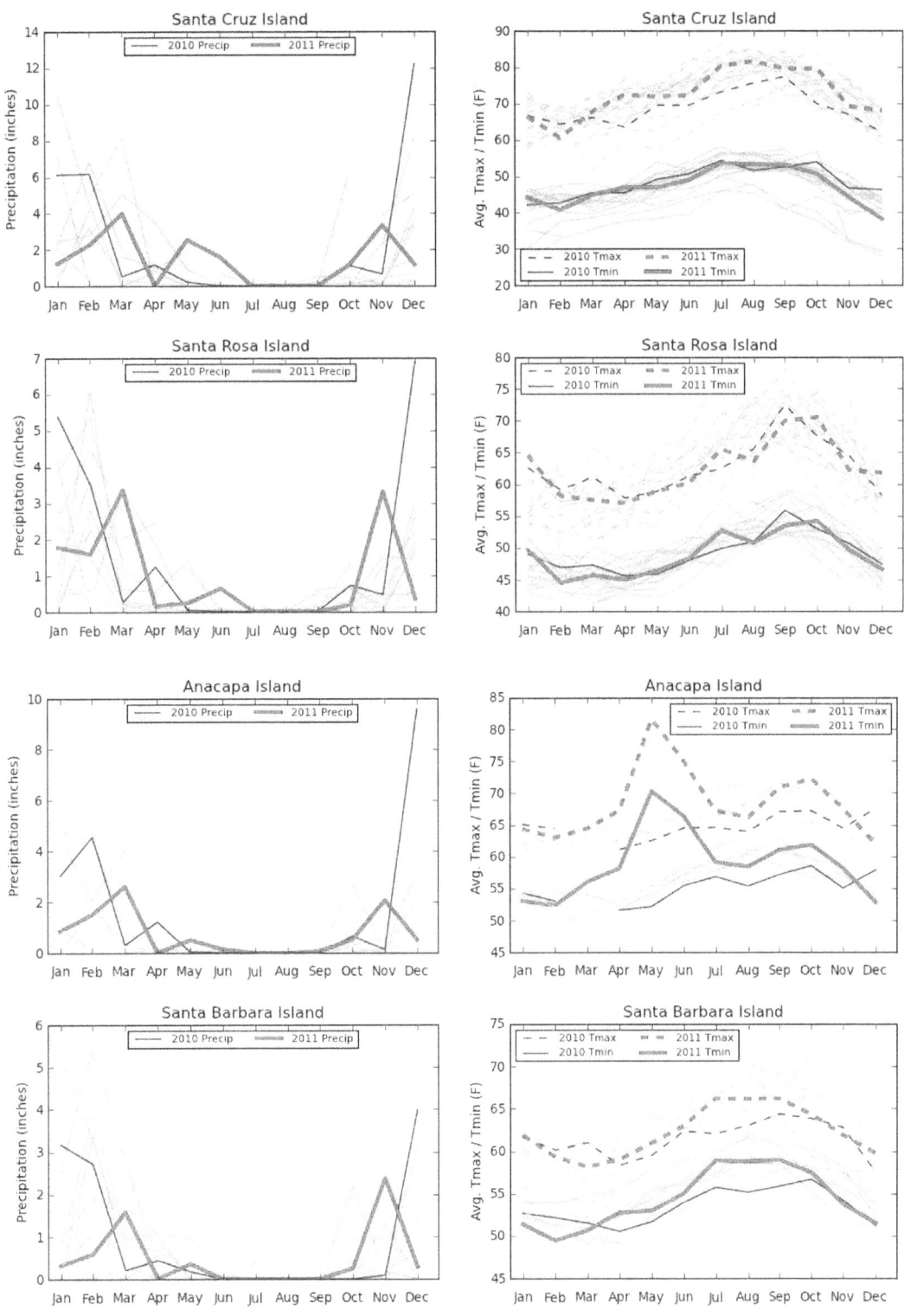

Figure 8. Total monthly precipitation, average daily maximum temperature (Tmax), and average daily minimum temperature (Tmin) for the period of record at automated (RAWS) stations in Channel Islands National Park. Calendar year 2011 is shown in red and 2010 is shown in blue. All earlier years are shown as gray lines. RAWS stations have not been in operation long enough to calculate 30-year averages so the difference between the current year and other years is shown qualitatively rather than as in Fig. 7 for NWS stations.

19

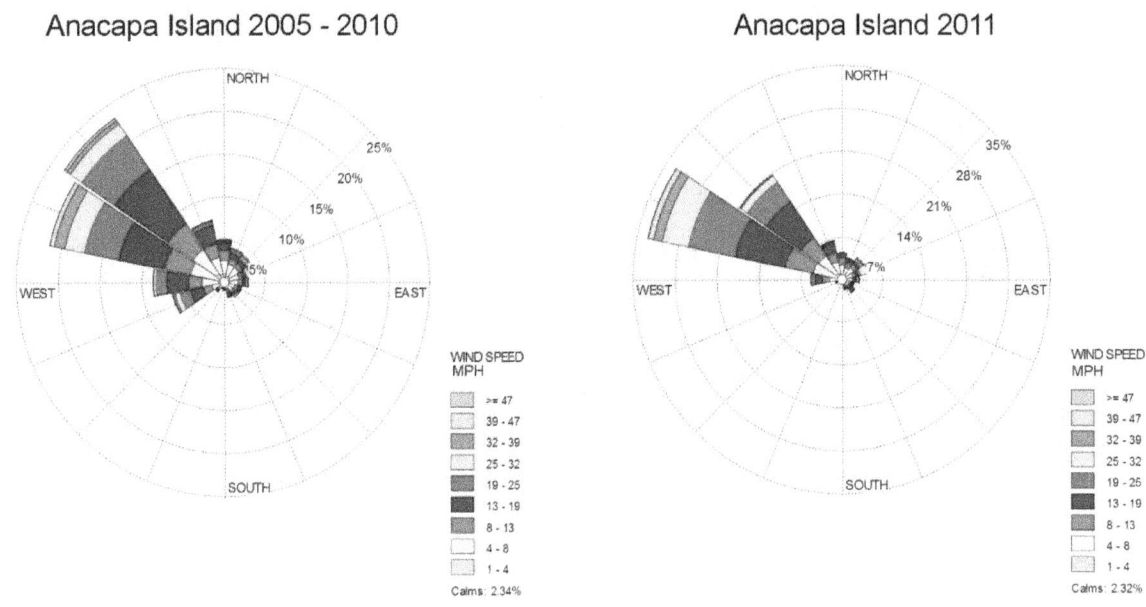

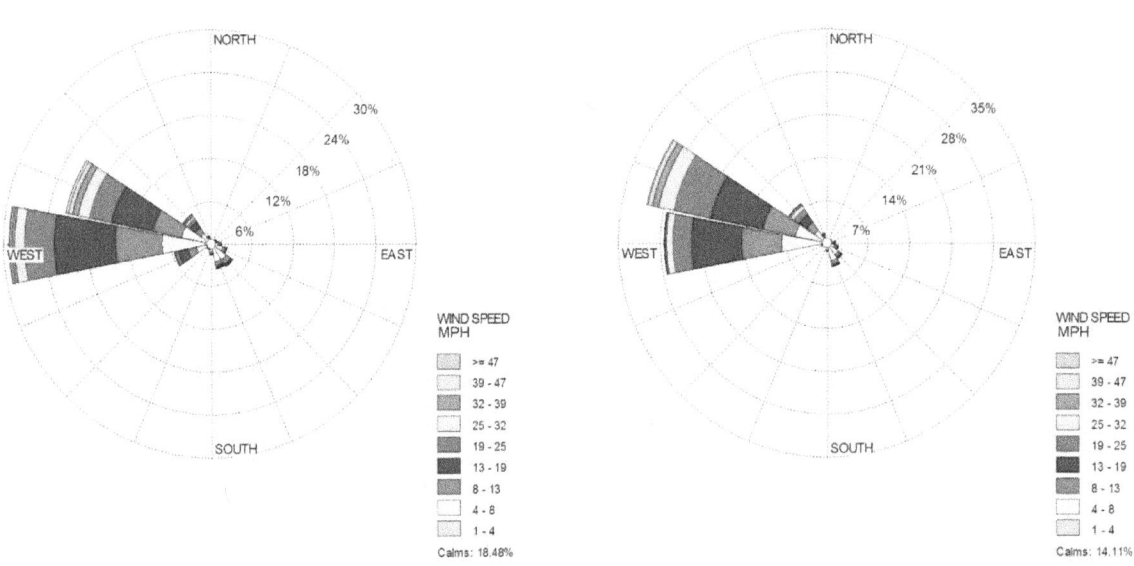

Figure 9. Wind roses for RAWS stations in Channel Islands National Park, contrasting calendar year 2011 to the averages for 2005 – 2010. The orientation of a spoke indicates wind direction (compass heading, degrees from which the wind originated), and the length of a spoke indicates the amount of time (%) that wind from a given direction occurred. Colors within the spokes express the amount of time (%) that wind from each direction had the indicated velocity.

20

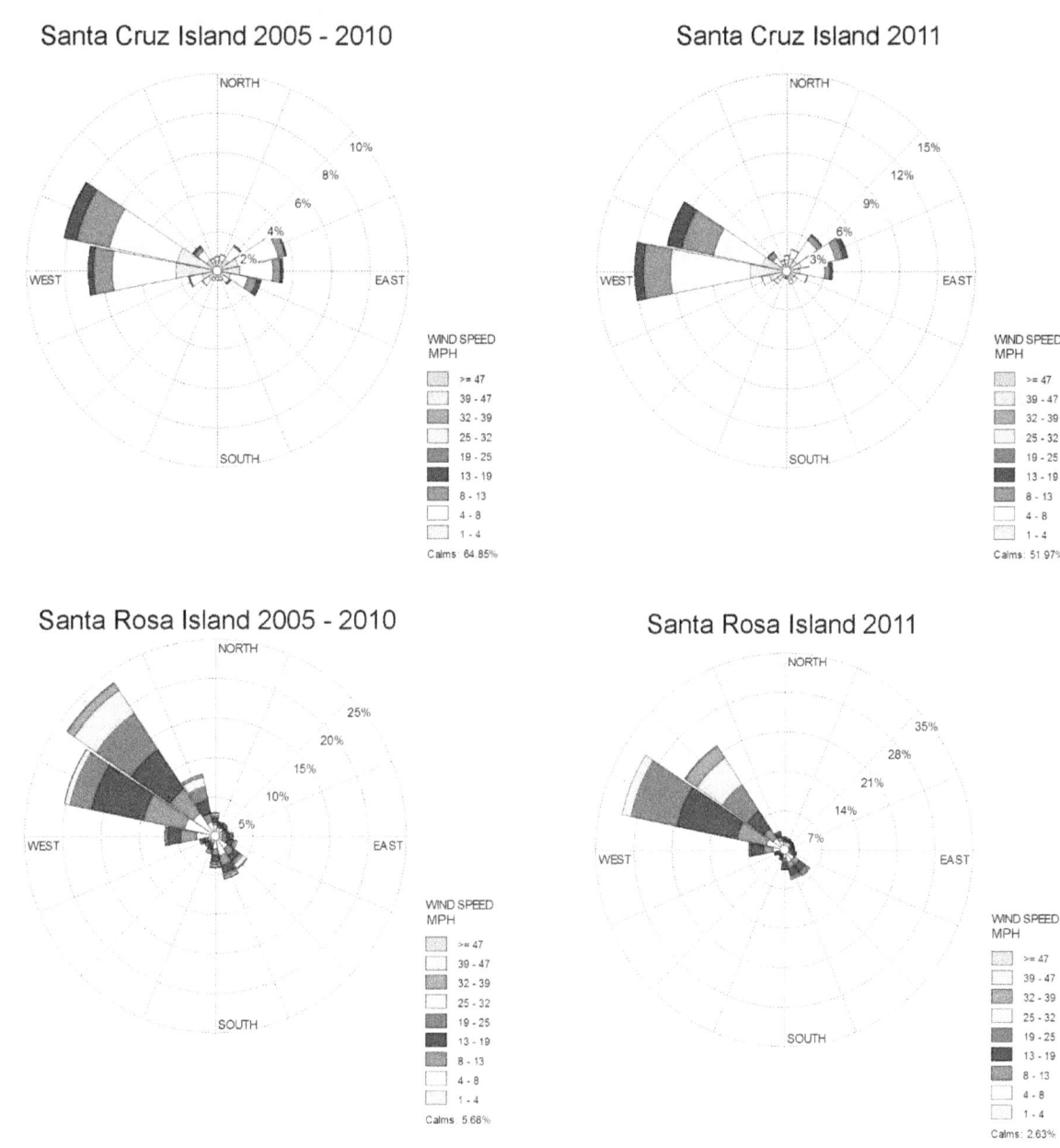

Figure 9. Continued.

21

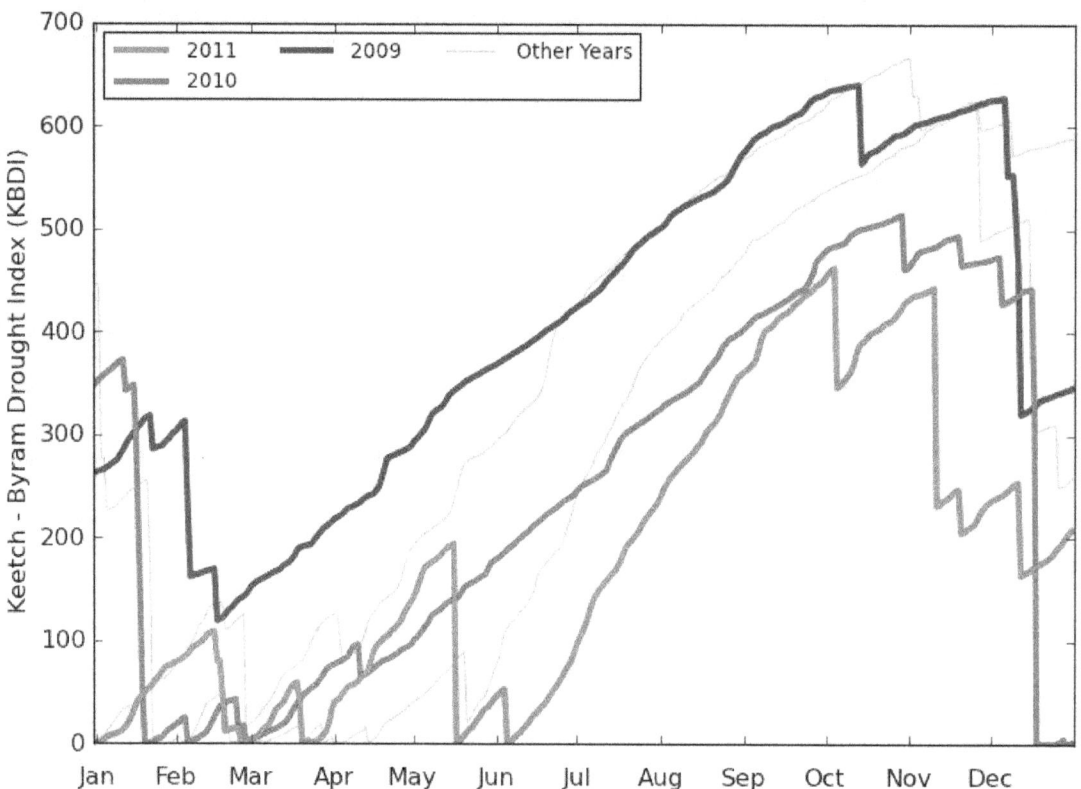

Figure 10. The Keetch-Byram Drought Index (KBDI) calculated for every day during the period of record for the Santa Cruz Island weather station. The maximum value possible for KBDI is 800, which would indicate that 8 hundredths of an inch (8 inches) of water would be required to replenish the soil to field capacity. The data quality criteria for calculation of KBDI are stringent, so it was only possible to calculate the index for 6 years of data. Nevertheless, the patterns shown here were the same for the other stations in Channel Islands National Park and for stations on the mainland.

22

Conclusions

- The region recovered from drought during 2010, and remained drought free during 2011.
- A strong La Nina did not produce the expected dry winter in southern California during the winter of 2010 – 2011. December 2010 was much wetter than average, and the Channel Islands had a wetter than normal spring.
- June precipitation on Santa Cruz Island was 3100% the 1981 – 2010 average. It was the third wettest June since records began in 1904. January, April, September and December had well below average precipitation. Other months had precipitation near or slightly above the 30-year averages.
- Temperatures during 2011 were generally near to below 1981 – 2010 averages.
- Wind patterns were not out of the ordinary and fire risk was low.

Literature Cited

Alexander, M.E. 1990. Computer calculation of the Keetch-Byram Drought Index – programmers beware. Fire management notes 51(4): 23 – 25.

Daly, C., M. Halbleib, J. I. Smith, W. P. Gibson, M. K. Doggett, G. H. Taylor, J. Curtis, and P. P. Pasteris. 2008. Physiographically sensitive mapping of climatological temperature and precipitation across the conterminous United States. International Journal of Climatology 28(15): 2031–2064.

Dolling, K., P. Chu, and F. Fujioka. 2005. A climatological study of the Keetch/Byram drought index and fire activity in the Hawaiian Islands. Agricultural and Forest Meteorology 133: 17 – 27.

Keetch, J.J. and G.M. Byram. 1968. A drought index for forest fire control. USDA Forest Service Research Paper SE-38.

Kittel, T. 2008. The Development and Analysis of Climate Datasets for National Park Science and Management: A Guide to Methods for Making Climate Records Useful and Tools to Explore Critical Questions. Report prepared for the National Park Service Inventory and Monitoring Program. University of Colorado, Institute of Arctic and Alpine Research, Boulder, Colorado, USA.

Kittel, T., S. Ostermann-Kelm, B. Frakes, M. Tercek, S. Gray, and C. Daly. 2009. A framework for climate analysis and reporting for Greater Yellowstone (GRYN) and Rocky Mountain (ROMN) networks: A report from the GRYN/ROMN climate data analysis workshop, Bozeman, Montana, 7–8 April 2009. Final draft. Prepared for the National Park Service, Greater Yellowstone Inventory and Monitoring Program, Bozeman, Montana, USA.

Rocky Mountain Climate Working Group. 2010. Rocky Mountain climate protocol: Climate monitoring in the Greater Yellowstone and Rocky Mountain inventory and monitoring networks, Version 1.0. Natural Resource Report NPS/IMRO/NRR—2010/222. National Park Service, Fort Collins, Colorado.

Tercek, M.T. 2011. Channel Islands National Park – Climate of 2010. Report Submitted to the National Park Service Mediterranean Coast Inventory and Monitoring Network.

Appendix 1

Table of climate stations used in this report. Detailed histories, period of record, and 30-year averages can be accessed from the links provided.

Name	Stn type	Metadata
Santa Rosa Island "Black Mountain" (NPS)	RAWS	http://www.wrcc.dri.edu/cgi-bin/rawMAIN.pl?caCSRI
Santa Cruz Island "Main Ranch" (NPS)	RAWS	http://www.wrcc.dri.edu/cgi-bin/rawMAIN.pl?caCSCI
Anacapa Island (NPS)	RAWS	http://www.wrcc.dri.edu/cgi-bin/rawMAIN.pl?caCANA
Santa Barbara Island ((NPS)	RAWS	http://www.wrcc.dri.edu/cgi-bin/rawMAIN.pl?caCSBB
Santa Cruz Island "Main Ranch" (manual)	Manual	http://www.wrcc.dri.edu/cgi-bin/cliMAIN.pl?ca7802+sca
Santa Rosa Island	Manual	http://www.wrcc.dri.edu/cgi-bin/cliMAIN.pl?ca7804+sca
Santa Barbara Island	Manual	http://www.wrcc.dri.edu/cgi-bin/cliMAIN.pl?ca7801+sca

Appendix 2

Monthly wind roses for RAWS Stations in Channel Islands NP during 2011.

Anacapa Island

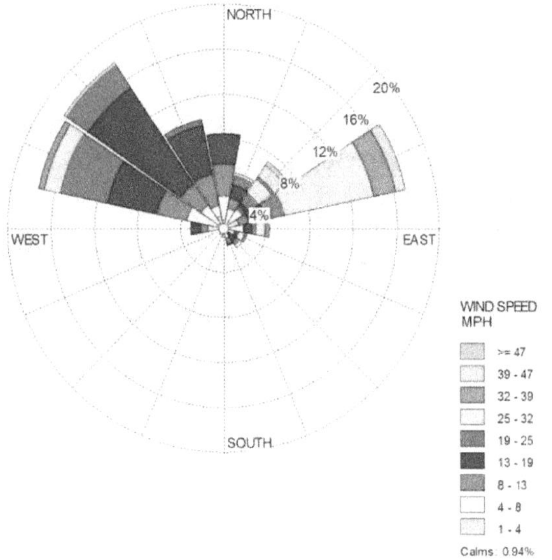

January

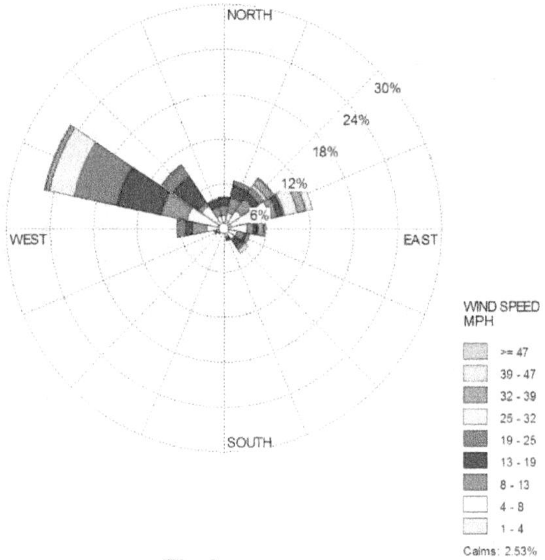

February

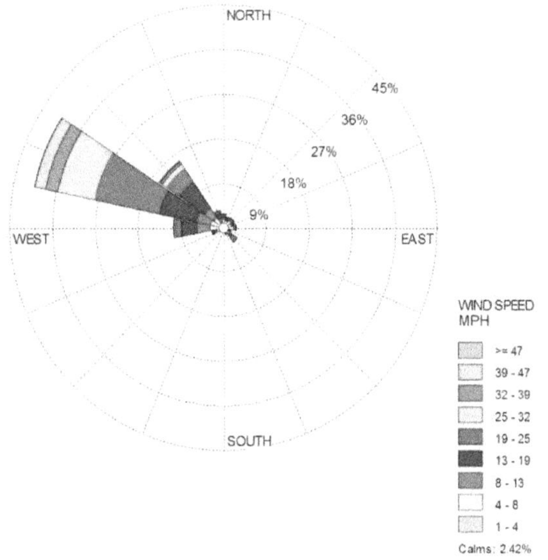

March

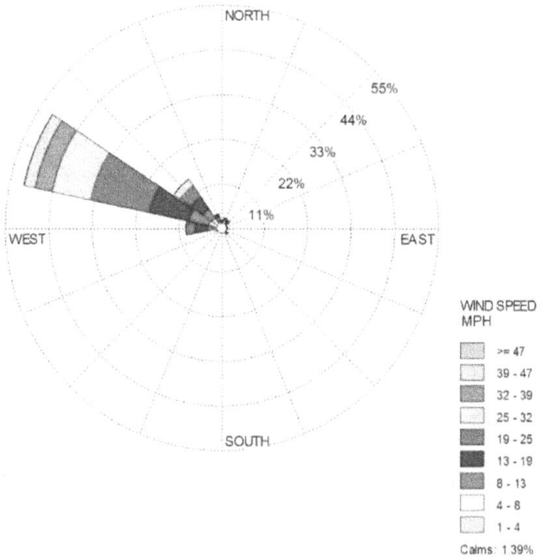

April

Anacapa Island

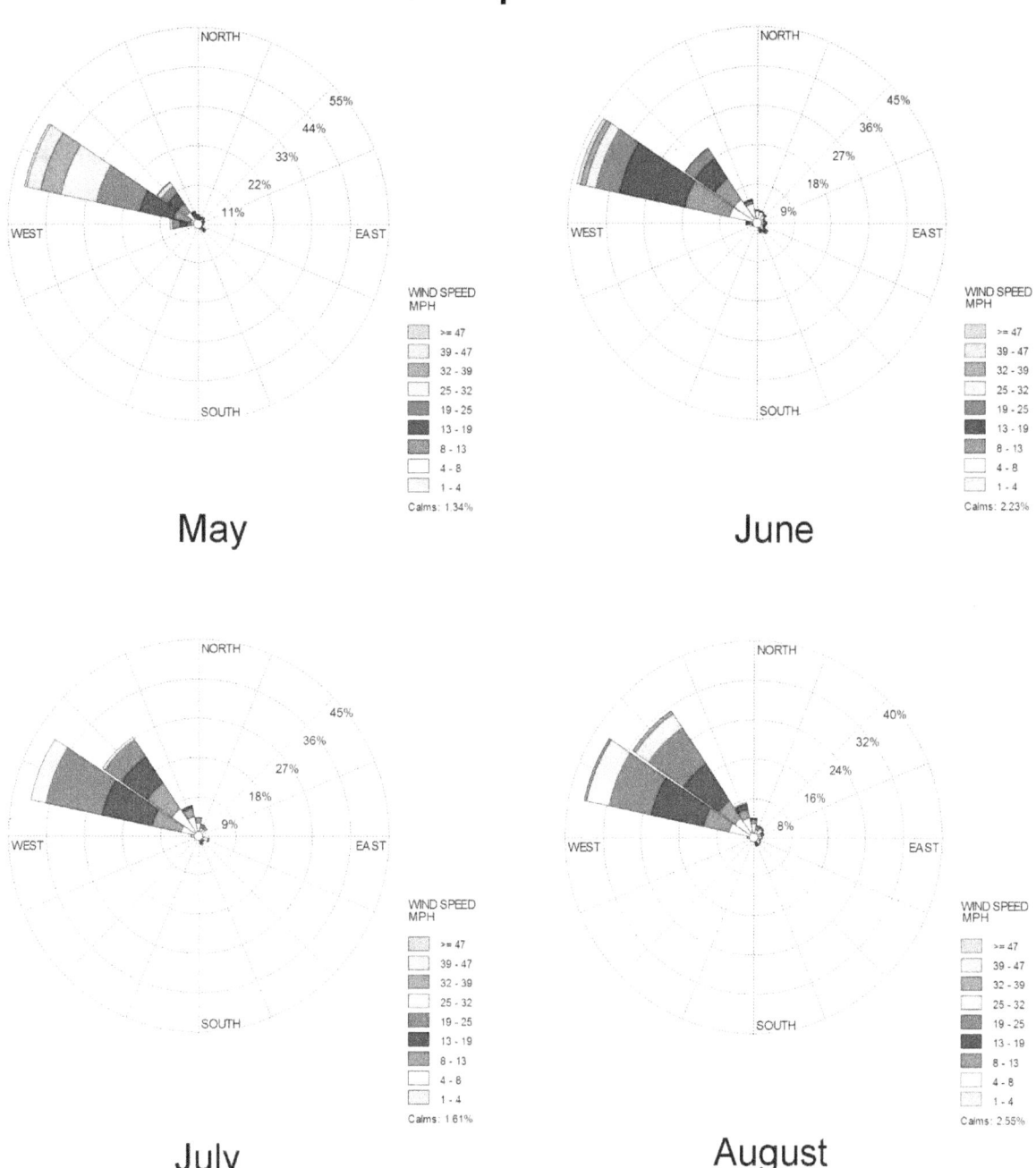

May

June

July

August

Anacapa Island

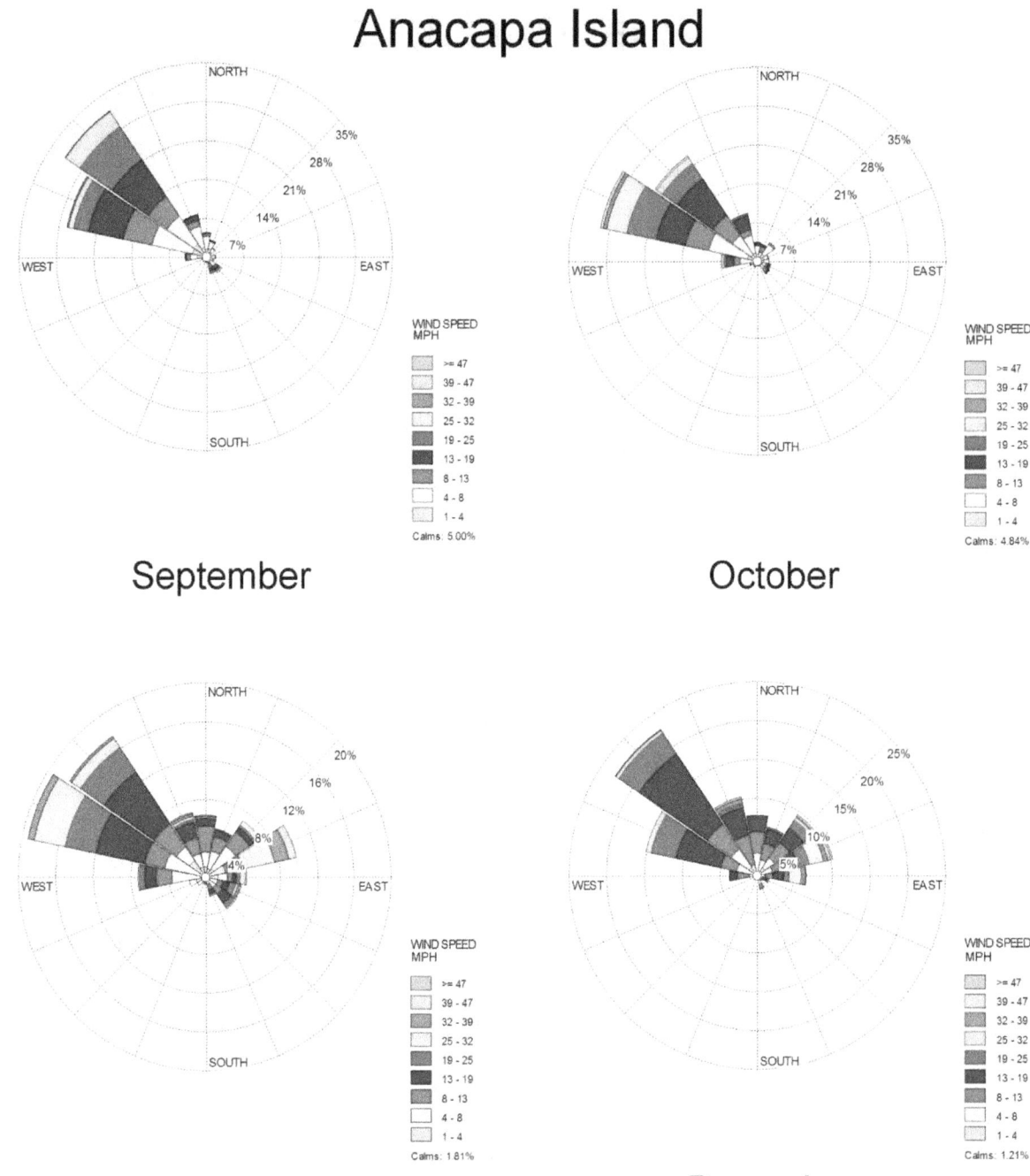

September

October

November

December

Santa Barbara Island

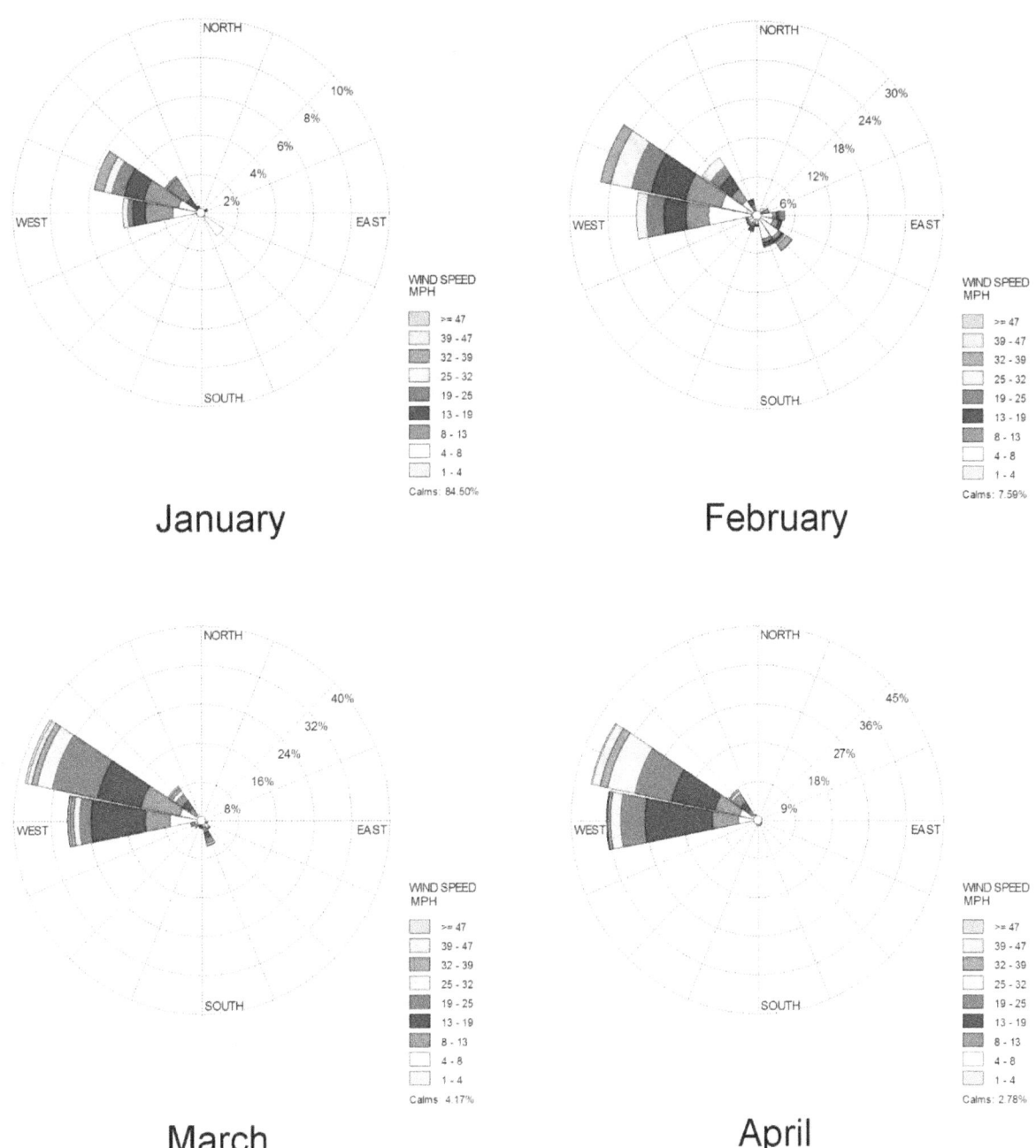

January

February

March

April

Santa Barbara Island

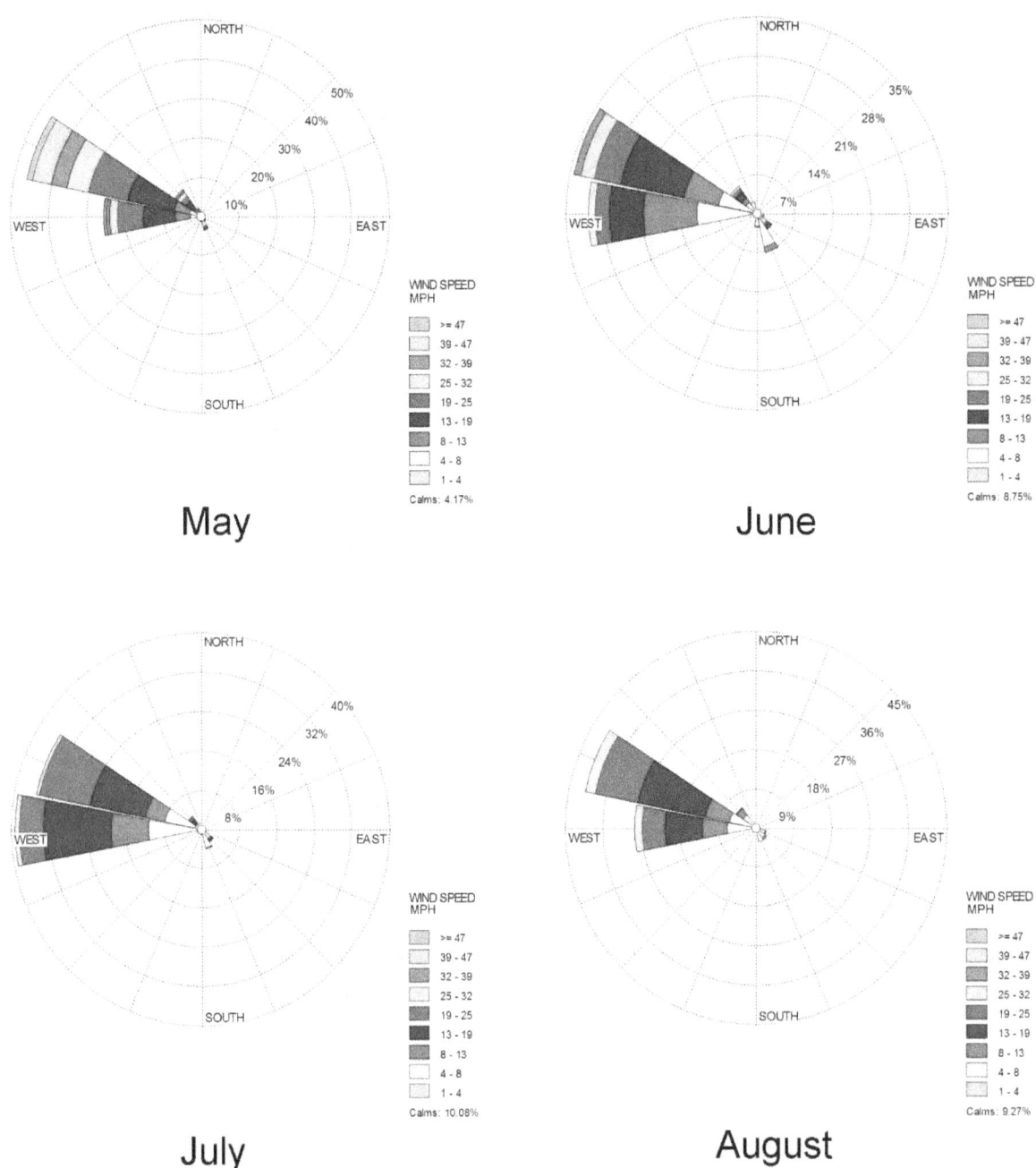

May

June

July

August

Santa Barbara Island

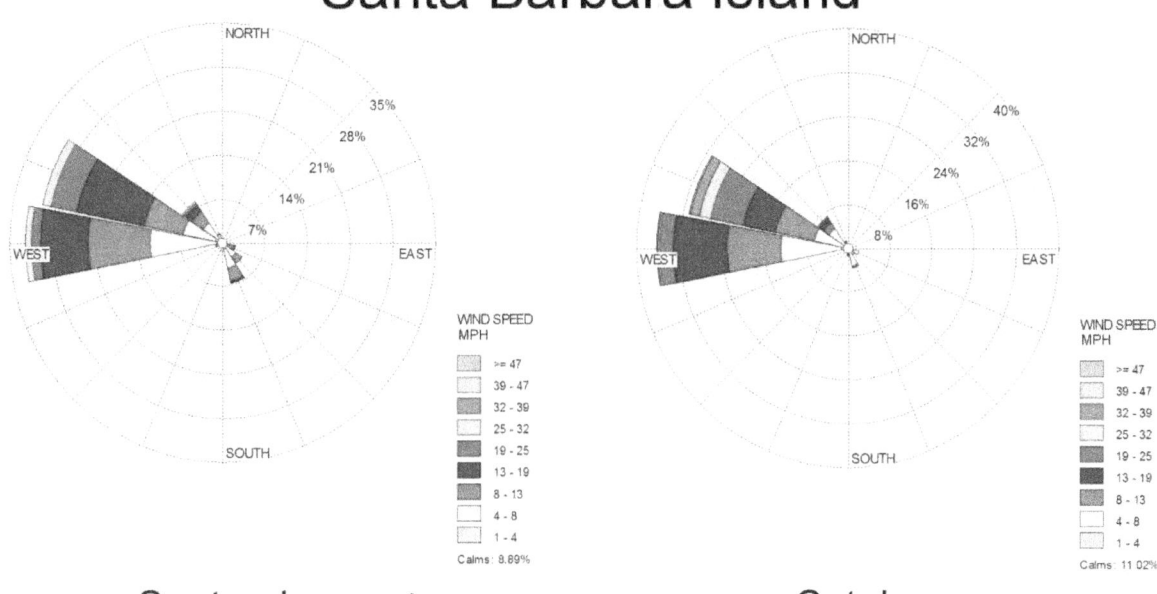

September

October

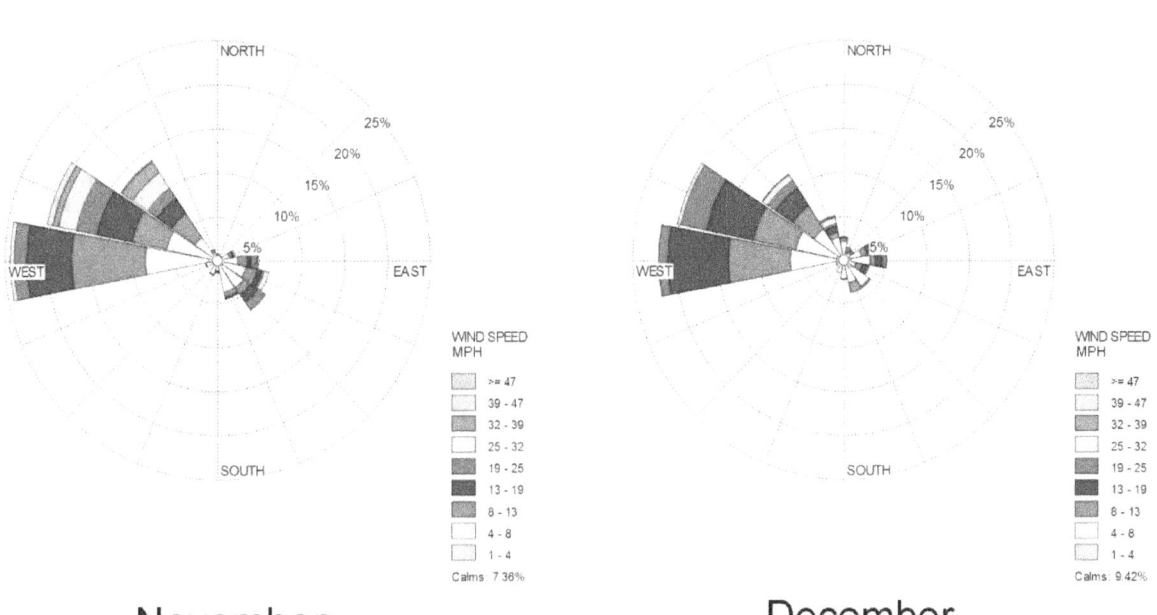

November

December

Santa Cruz Island

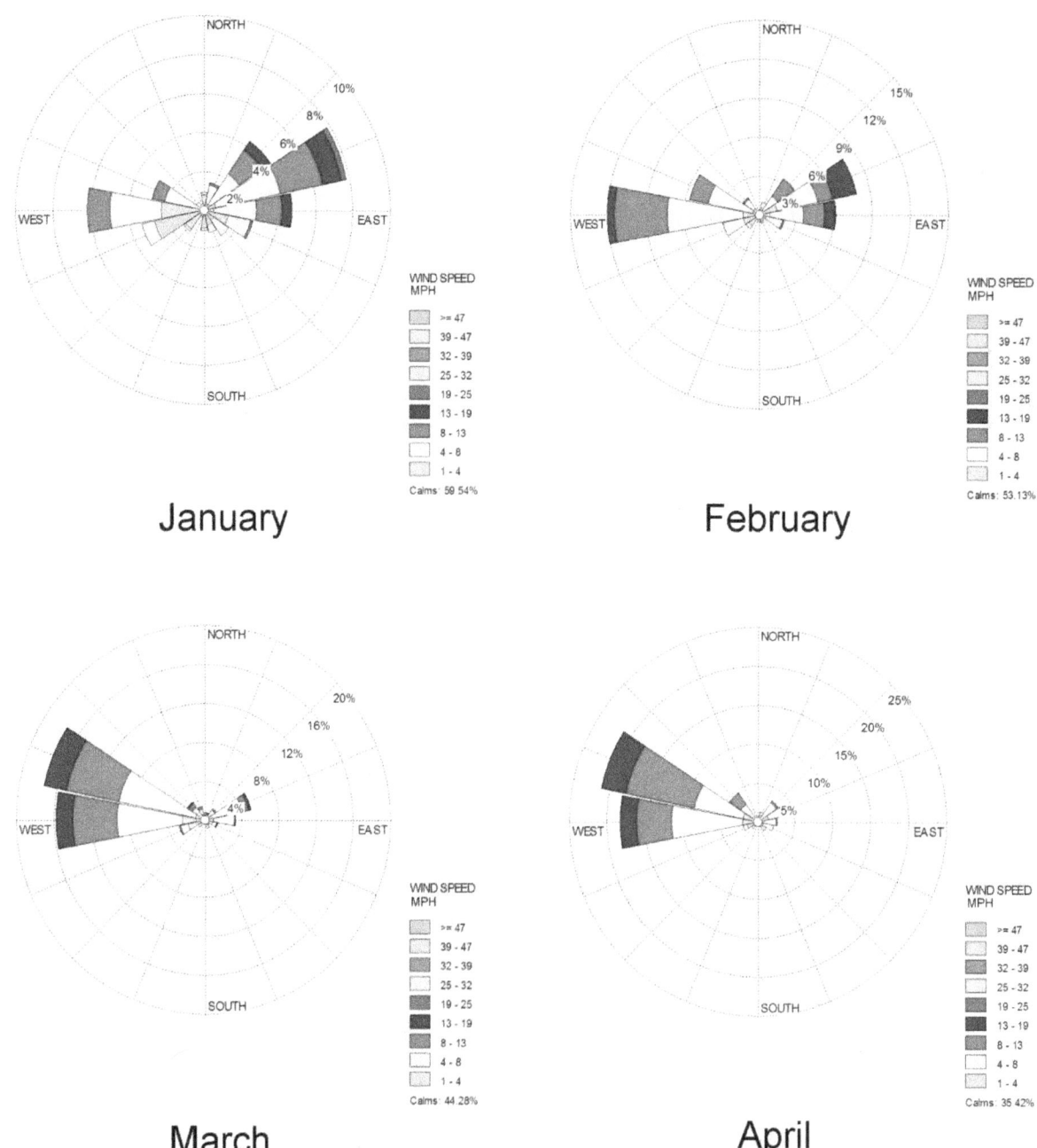

January

February

March

April

Santa Cruz Island

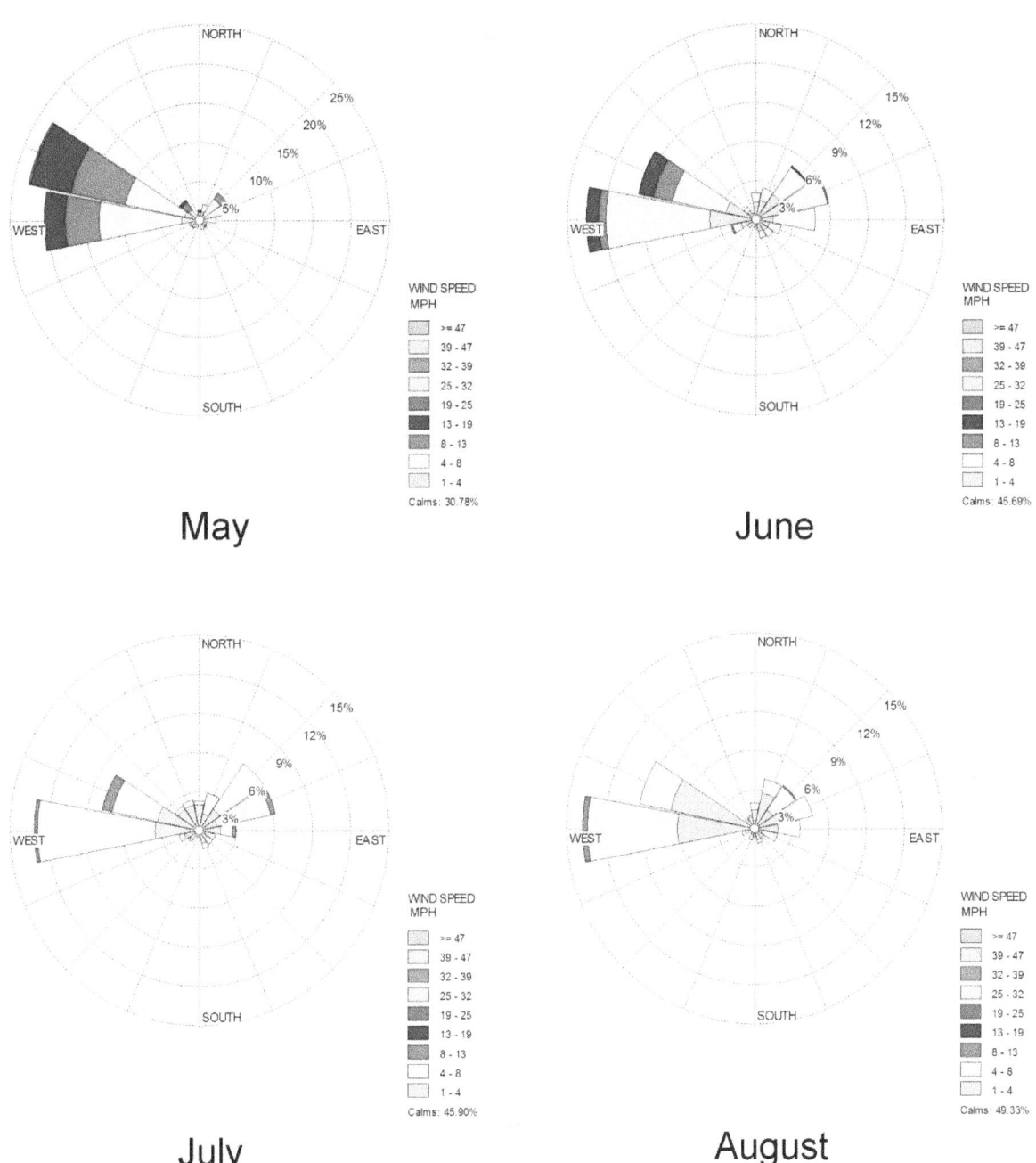

May

June

July

August

Santa Cruz Island

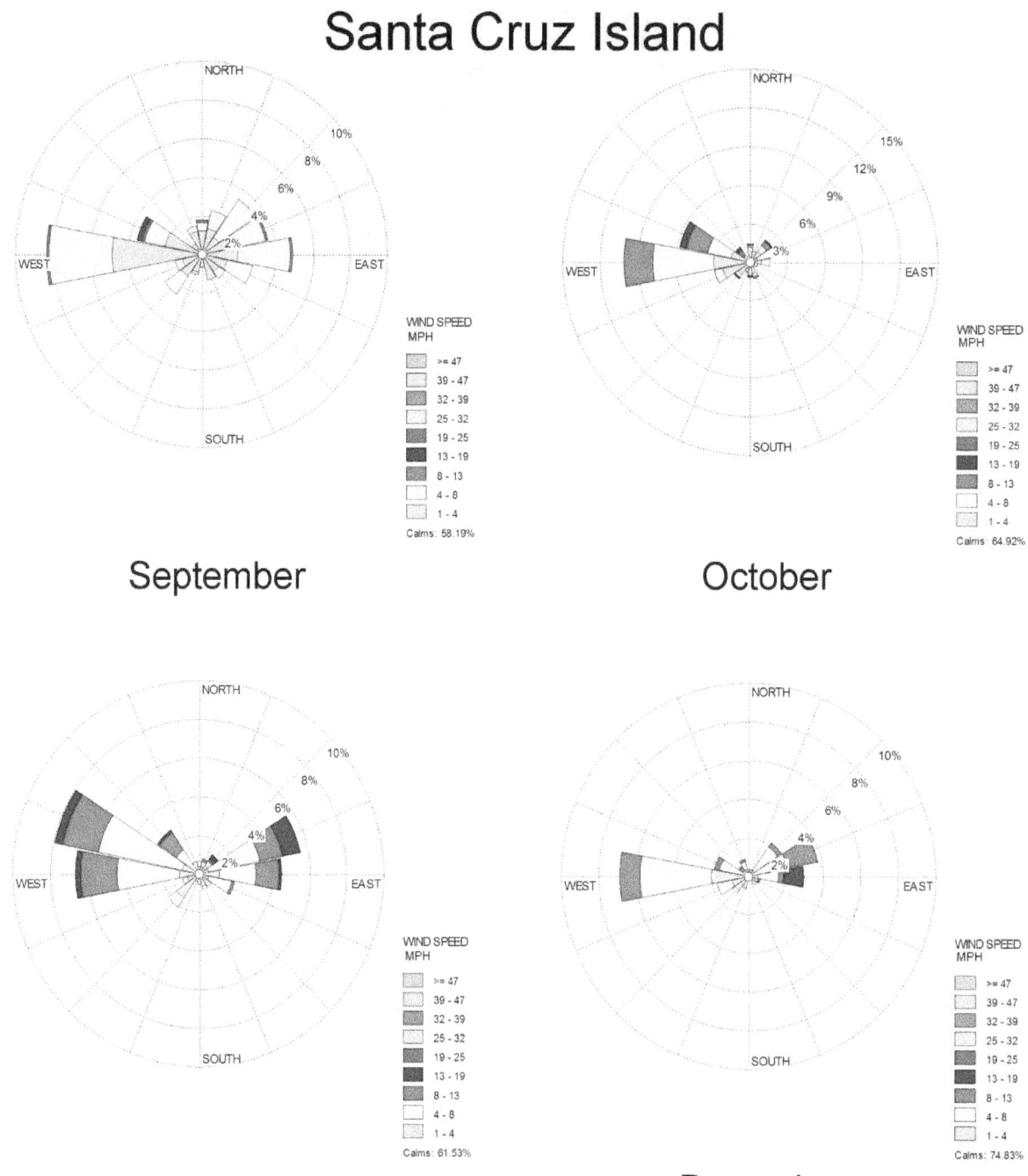

September

October

November

December

Santa Rosa Island

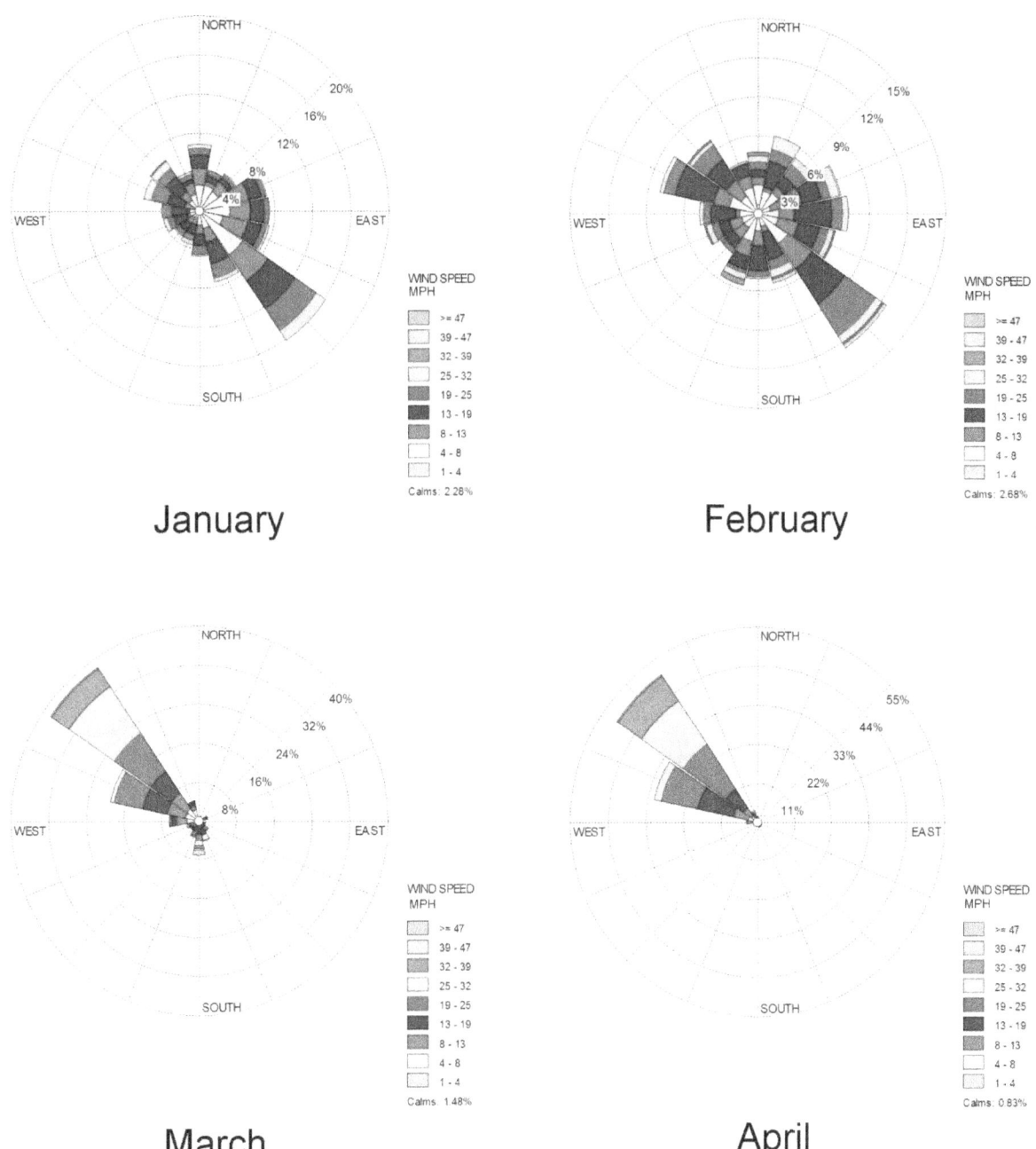

January

February

March

April

Santa Rosa Island

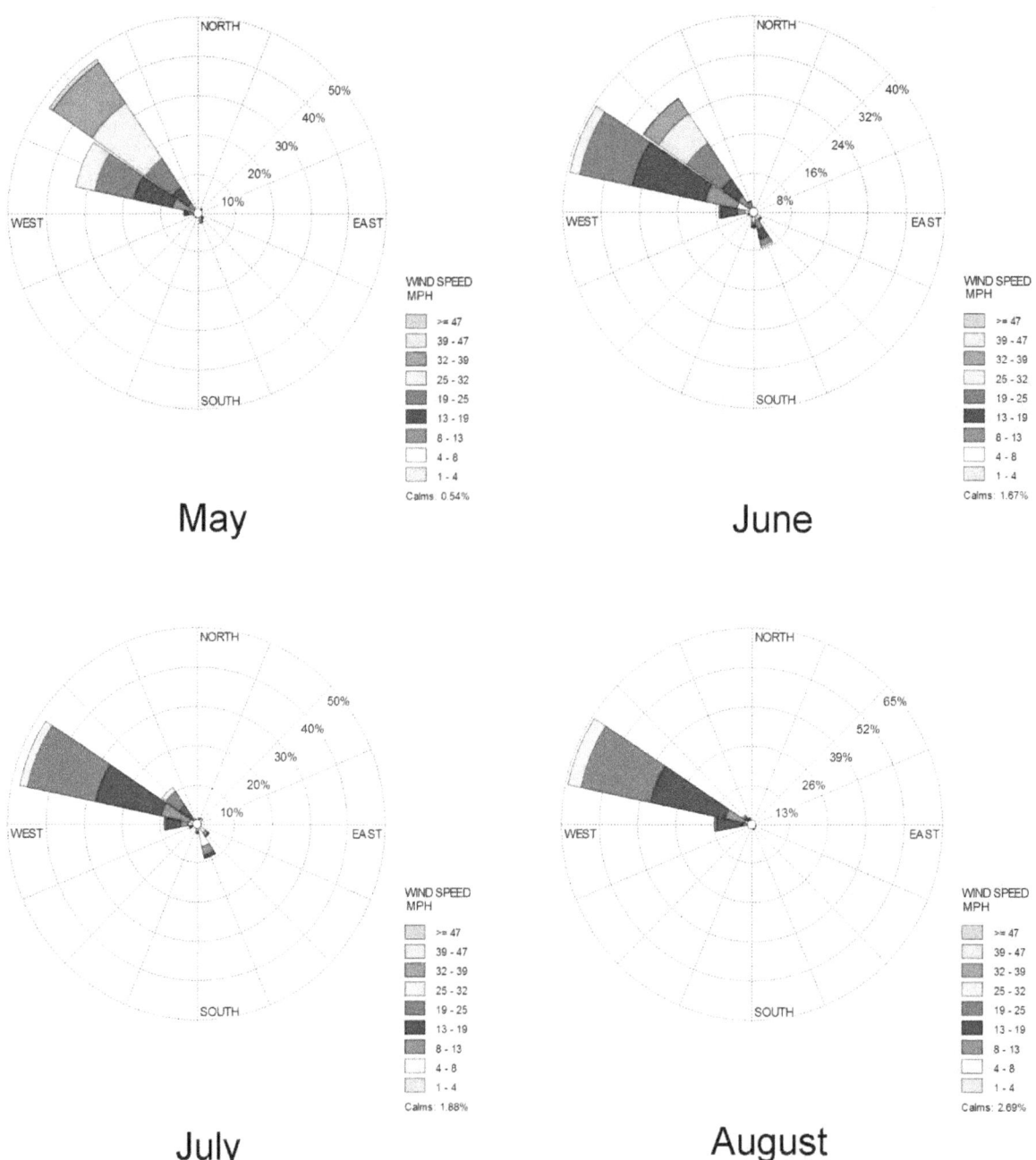

May

June

July

August

Santa Rosa Island

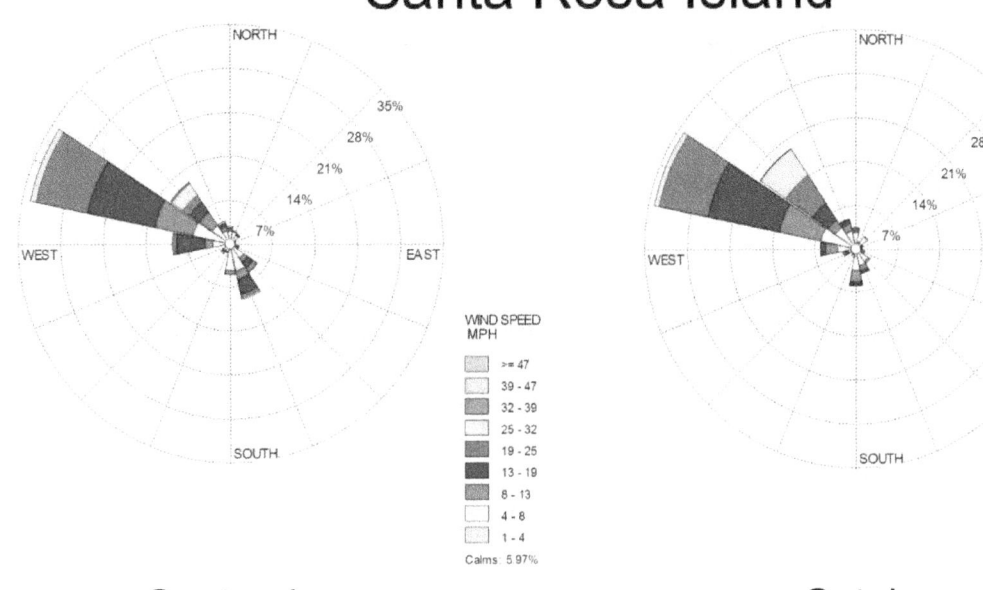

September

October

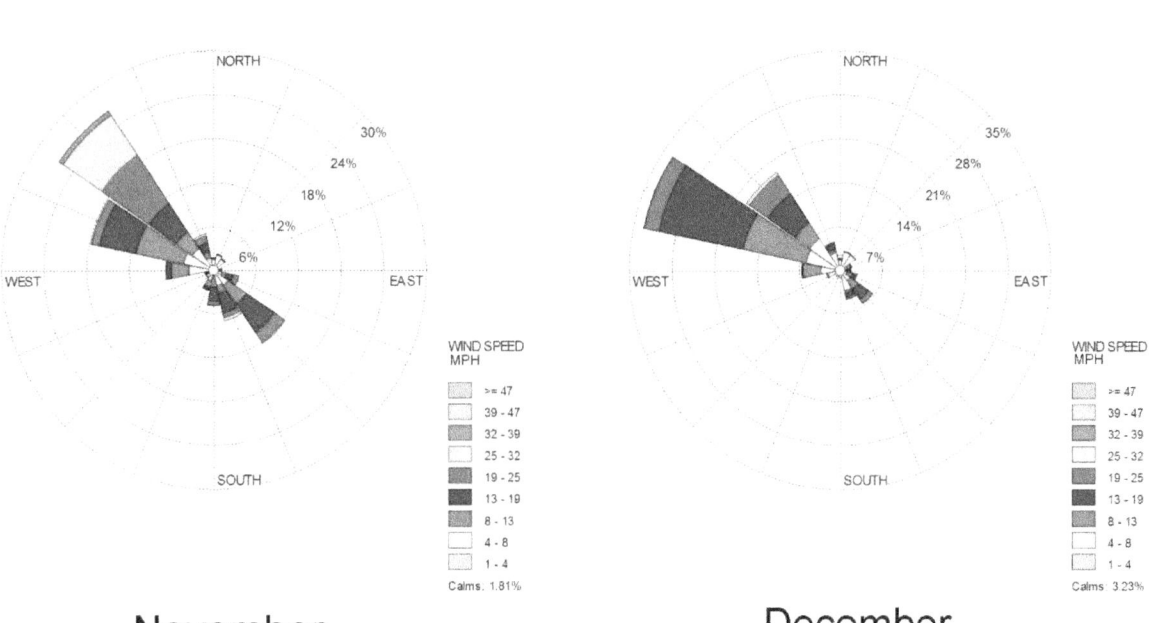

November

December

Appendix 3

Comparison of Manual vs. Automated Precipitation Measurements on Santa Cruz, Santa Rosa and Santa Barbara Islands

A comparison of monthly precipitation totals at the automated (RAWS) vs. manual ("Ranger") weather stations shows the best agreement on Santa Cruz Island, and the agreement between the two stations is better from 2006 – present (see the figure below). In contrast, precipitation measurements at the Santa Rosa Island manual station were significantly greater than at the automated station. There was insufficient data in the manual record to make an accurate comparison on Santa Barbara Island. Figure 9 illustrates the differences just described.

On Santa Cruz Island during the period 1990 – 2011, simple addition of months in which measurements were available from both weather stations yields 195.11 inches at the RAWS station and 207.97 inches at the manual station. Based on these numbers, it is estimated that the automated station records roughly 94% the precipitation recorded at the manual station. Note that since these totals were calculated only for months in which both stations had recorded values, they are not accurate precipitation totals for the period 1990 – 2011. They were calculated only for purposes of comparison between the two weather stations. There were many months during this period in which only one of either the manual or RAWS weather station had recorded data.

On Santa Rosa Island, totals for months in which both stations made measurements were 117.15 inches at the automated station and 190.85 inches at the manual station. Based on this, it is estimated that the automated station records roughly 61% the precipitation that is measured by the manual station.

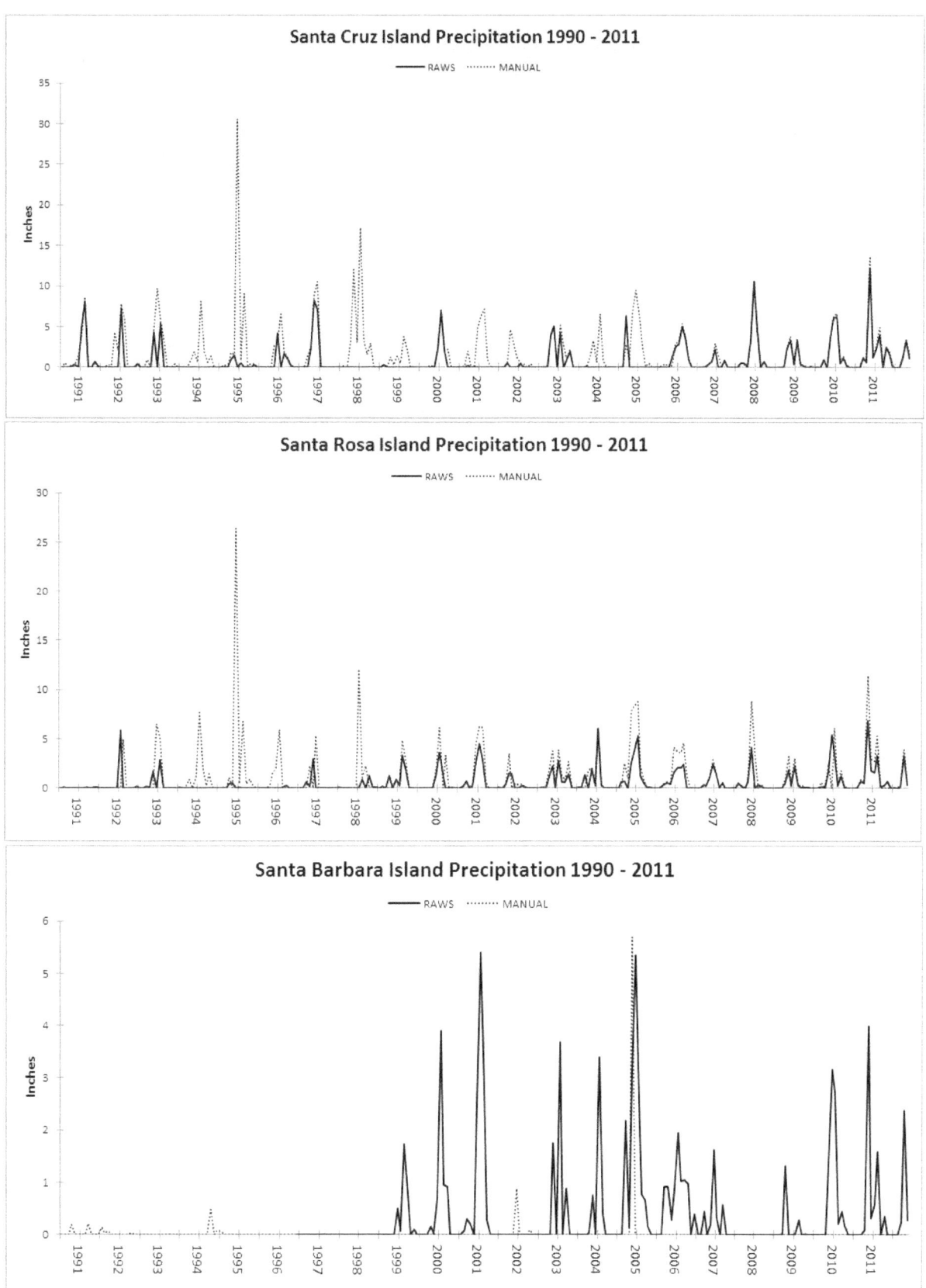

Appendix 3, Figure 1. Comparison of precipitation measurements from manual vs. automated weather stations in Channel Islands National Park.